The Fabian Sweater
(and other stories of a faulty memory)

A nostalgic look at growing up
in the 50's in Morris Cove

Ed Sabatino

Forward by:
Frank (Sonny) Anastasio
&
George (Greek) Pertesis

The Fabian Sweater (and other stories of a faulty memory)
By Ed Sabatino

Printed in the United States of America

ISBN 978-1-257-88021-8

All photos in this book were photographed by Anthony Sabatino

Dedication

This book is dedicated to my wife Barbara
and our three children, Jason, Eric and Lauren.
It's a book about happy times of days gone by.
But I wouldn't trade any of them for what I have now.

The stories in this book are true.
Any discrepancies are due to a vivid imagination
and a faulty memory.

Acknowledgments

A special thank you to my family and friends for taking the time to read and respond to what I'm sure they considered more of my silliness. I would also like to acknowledge "spell check" without who's help this book would have been a lot funnier.

Table of Contents

FORWARD

I moved to Morris Cove in 1959, a 13 year old somewhat quiet, somewhat insecure adolescent. I lived on Ley St, near Tweed New Haven Airport, right down the street from one of the hub areas of activity in Morris Cove. Nathan Hale School, Fort Hale Park, Ralph's Park Gate Spa and Greek's wall. Everyone who lived in Morris Cove knew where these places were.

Morris Cove is probably not unlike thousands of places in the United States where families live and kids grow up; where people work and kids play baseball; where people fall in love and have children. Of course, if it is where YOU grew up, it is special and unique.

The Cove, as we called it, is geographically on the east shore of New Haven, CT. It is beautifully caressed by Long Island Sound at the entrance to New Haven harbor. It has parks and beaches and landmarks that became fixtures in our lives. The basketball courts, the "spa" and "the park" became the places we met, hung out, socialized and played.

The Cove was primarily a residential area of mostly one family homes. It had some small family owned businesses like Betty's store and Ralph's Spa, but no large shopping centers. It had two schools – Nathan Hale and St.

Bernadettes. The Cove is just about the same today in 2011 as it was in 1959.

At 13, I had all the awkwardness and insecurities than many teenagers experience. I was unsure how to act around girls, worried about getting pimples and trying to figure out that ultimate balancing act – to be independent of my parent's expectations and at the same time trying to please them.

The Cove was the perfect place to discover yourself, to form your own identity. There were plenty of fantastic people to make friends with and loads of recreational opportunities. School systems were good. Most parents of friends opened their doors and welcomed you into their family with support. You could really feel part of a community in the Cove.

In 1959, economically, our country was in good shape. If you wanted to make money you could. I remember clearly how proud I was one day when a friend and I each made $100 shoveling snow from neighborhood walkways. For a young teen in 1959, that was a lot of money (and a lot of work). Having a little cash in your pocket was important when you wanted to be "grown up".

It's 2011 now. I have recently renewed some wonderful friendships of 50 years ago and of course a good deal of the conversation we have is of the Cove years. I guess when you hit the "senior citizen" years, you become a little more nostalgic.

Why I am telling all of this to you? My purpose is to set the stage for the main event – a story beautifully and skillfully told by Ed Sabatino. In the following chapters, Ed will share many of his Cove life experiences with insight, honesty and, of course, a sense of humor. Ed was known for his comedic talents. He was fun to be around, always ready with something funny to say or do. But he could be serious too. Ed is an artist. He did pen and ink drawings, especially caricatures, that were fantastic. He and I are married to the best-friend-teenage-girls who we met together in a little restaurant where I worked at age eighteen. We "double dated", had loads of fun and started families together. Today Ed is a pastor in a church in Florida. I'm sure he must bring some smiles and laughter to his congregation just as he did with his friends in the 1960s.

One of the country music hits of this year is a song by Miranda Lambert called "The House that Built Me". She sings about returning to her childhood home to try to find herself, perhaps looking for some meaning from the past. Sometimes we can get in touch with who we *are* by getting in touch with who we *were* in our younger years.   When I reminisce about the Cove, I often think of those years as the "house that built me". In the following pages, Ed is describing the "house that built him," and many of us.

We each have our own window on the world, each our different view and perspective of life's events. Ed artfully describes his unique look at the Cove years and I'm sure it will get us in touch with our own memories of some of the great Cove days.

Frank (Sonny) Anastasio
June 2011

FORWARD

When Ed asked if I would want to write a blurb or two about growing up in the Morris Cove section of New Haven I was at once both honored and concerned. Honored that he would ask me for my thoughts but concerned as to how to write a Forward about a terrific childhood environment without presenting an idealized portrait that is far from reality. To be sure, there are shore side places that are as good to grow up in but none any better than the Cove.

Morris Cove, located on the eastern shore of New Haven, is a large primarily residential area, bordered on the west by New Haven harbor, Long Island Sound to the south, and Tweed airport and East Haven to the east. The Cove unofficially begins at the Hall Street/Fort Hale Road area and winds its way south and east towards the "Sound" and East Haven, terminating at Lighthouse Park and Morgan Point, East Haven. It remains populated, culturally and economically, by moderate to middle class blue and white collared families with an occasional household of established wealth thrown in for good measure. Most of the homes were and still are single family, owner occupied. Some families have resided there for multiple generations; such is their love for and contentment with the Cove.

The pre-teen years had a sense of security and exploration in this vast play area comprised of the local marina, Fort Hale Park, the moat with its caves, the Seawall, the beaches, Nathan Hale School yard and the ball fields. The teenage years were wrought with the hopes and sometimes the actuality of early romantic entanglements. At a quick count there must have been 50 to 80 or more sets of siblings spaced about 4 years apart….those conceived or born prior to their dads going off to World War II and those born after dads came home from wartime service. Ah, the baby boom generation had arrived. There were so many of us that each block was its own distinct micro neighborhood with its own focus and orientation, yet, we were able to go from street to street and fit in. There was a real comfort in that. School and chores notwithstanding, we played all morning, afternoon and evening and at night, after a strenuous day playing, many of us could lie back in our beds and listen to the waves lapping at the shores of the Cove.

As with much of post war America, dads went off to work each day and many moms worked outside the home while still making sure we had our cookies and milk after school. Our parents certainly sacrificed to provide us with an environment and opportunity for a terrific childhood. Similar to other areas during the 50's and 60's each Cove kid had multiple "moms" who were inclined to admonish you if you were caught doing something you shouldn't have been doing....our own built in policing force.

This is the environment in which Ed grew up and so easily chronicles. The stories Ed writes speak to the very nature of Morris Cove. The family structures, the neighborhoods and the characters inhabiting them, the skills and understandings gained from competitive sports, and the hopes, desires and fears of the teenage years are all woven together into a fabric that depicts growing up in the Cove. I can think of no one more engaging to write about events, personal or otherwise, occurring there during the 50's and 60's. It is so easy to visualize what he writes.
From my perspective, Ed has approached so many things in life with such energy, clarity and self-deprecating humor that I often think he is living and telling a Gene Shepard story. Happy reading!

George (Greek) Pertesis

Introduction

Hugging the eastern shore of New Haven Harbor lies the coastal town of Morris Cove. Originally part of the town of East Haven Connecticut, Morris Cove was named for one of its early settlers Thomas Morris. With its picturesque tree lined streets and beachfront homes its the ideal place to grow up. No matter where you live you are within walking distance to Long Island Sound, The Seawall, Fort Hale Park and Lighthouse State Park.

My house was on the corner of Ira and Burr Street. My Grandmother lived directly across the street with my Aunt Mary. There were other relatives scattered around the neighborhood to numerous to mention. On holidays the entire family would get together at one of our houses and have a feast that would rival that of King Arthur's court. The grown ups would sit around the table for the entire day, telling stories, drinking wine, and cracking walnuts. We ate at the "kids table."

There is a myth about the 1950's. That decade is looked upon as a time of innocence, where people lived an idealistic existence without a care in the world. Nothing could be farther from the truth. People had just as many problems then as they do now, maybe even more. There were racial tensions, the threat of nuclear war as well as the everyday anxieties of raising a family and making a living. But for a kid growing up in Morris Cove, those things never touched our lives. For us it really was a time of innocence, for us it really was a different world.

It was the simple things that made it so different and so wonderful. Kids would play outside until supper and no one ever gave it a second thought. Milk was delivered to our house in glass bottles. We ate TV Dinners in tin trays. Gas was 17 cents a gallon and that included cleaning the windshield, checking the oil and green stamps. Mothers hung the wash outside on a cloths line. Doors were never locked, and phone numbers had a "prefix" and a party line. Kids would occupy themselves for hours at a time playing Hide and Seek, 1-2-3 Red Light, Hop Scotch, and Jump Rope. Sometimes on warm summer afternoons we would lie on our backs and see pictures in the clouds. At night we would catch fireflies in a jar as the sound of crickets filled the air. When we got thirsty we took a drink from the garden hose and we rode each other around on the handlebars of our bicycles.

We ate candy cigarettes. Played with cap guns and paint-by number paint sets. Roller skates had "keys." Girls wore poodle skirts and cars had fins. We went to 3-D movies and watched the news on TV which was only 15 minutes long and only gave the news, and just about the worst thing that could happen to a kid was getting picked last in a sandlot baseball game.

We had our pictures taken at a photo booth at Woolworths and they all looked like mug shots. Buster Brown he lived in a shoe, his dog Tag lived in there to. And every Sunday evening we heard that familiar voice from the Magic Kingdom say,

"Disneyland, each week as you enter this timeless land one of these many worlds will open to you. Frontierland. Tomorrowland. Adventureland and Fantasyland, the happiest kingdom of them all."

How true. Fantasyland is the happiest kingdom of all. But there is one more land I would like to add, Yesterdayland. I invite you to join me as I look back to my childhood and to that place that lies dormant in all of our lives...our youth.

Chapter One

Mayche And The Great Matchbook Caper

Someone once said, life is like a roll of toilet paper, the closer you get to the end the faster it goes. Rushing through my early teenage years such philosophical thoughts never entered my mind, I simply took each day as it came. Now, as I am approaching my "twilight years", that saying seems to hold a great amount of truth. The day's fly by like so many ants on a Ring Ding. But back in the 50's life was different.

Morris Cove was a small carefree community where everyone seemed to know one another. Located at the easternmost area of New Haven Harbor and Long Island Sound, the "Cove" included Fort Hale Park, and Lighthouse Point Park. There were plenty of places to swim, fish, and simply hang out. There were two churches, one Catholic and one Protestant. We had the same mailman for as long as I could remember. His name was Bob. Two grocery stores, Betty's and the A&P. One barber shop Al's, one cleaners, Lil's, a fire house, a liquor store and an airport. It was a simpler time. My main concerns were girls and pimples. I suppose the grown-ups had the same problems that we have today. Worries about paying bills, politics, and making a living, but those problems were light years away for a kid of 15.

The popular hangout at that time was a soda fountain, malt shop and convenient store combination called Ralph's Park Gate Spa. The words "Park Gate" were in reference to the store being located at the gate, or front entrance of Fort Hale Park, a great park complete with a small rocky beach, a playground for the kids, pavilions, a water fountain, a pier and even an initial tree. The proprietor, Ralph Turcio was a friendly man who had lived in Morris Cove all of his life . I'm sure he put up with a lot of aggravation from us kids but he never let it show. The Spa featured a magazine rack with all of the latest comic books, Archie, Casper, Little Audrey, Dare Devil as well as the daily newspapers. One of my earliest memories of The Spa was seeing the newspaper headline when the Yankees won the world series in 1956. Don Larsen pitched a no-hitter and the only perfect game in World Series history. I remember the picture on the front page of Yogi Berra jumping on Larson with his legs around his waist.

The Spa was sort of the mother planet, the gathering place, the hub of our activity. We would loiter around for hours at a time until Ralph finally had enough and threw us out. We would reluctantly leave only to return a few hours later. Of course one of the reasons Ralph became so frustrated with us is because we never spent a dime. Except maybe on the pinball machine. I remember when I was just a little squirt maybe 7 or 8, my father would give me $1.00 and send me to the Spa for two packs of Chesterfields. Ralph would hand them over no questions asked. As I said, it was a different time.

Ralph's Park Gate Spa was located right across the street from Saint Bernadette's Catholic Church. On Sunday mornings after Mass droves of people flocked into the Spa to buy the newspaper or some pastry. Ralph would always be in a good mood on Sundays as he stood behind the counter frantically trying to keep up with the customers. He reminded me of those plate jugglers we used to see on the Ed Sullivan Show, spinning five plates at a time and avoiding disaster at the last possible second. Somehow Ralph was able to keep up.

Winding along the shoreline along the harbor was The Sea Wall. An attractive little neighborhood park complete with benches and street lamps. A sidewalk and a wrought-iron fence lined the stone wall with several sets of steps that led down to the water. I loved to hear the sound of the waves as they flopped up against the steps. Morris Cove was a wonderful place to grow up. I remember lying in my bed on

Saturday nights listening to the distant sound of the stockcar races from across the harbor at Savin Rock as I drifted off to sleep. Sometimes the sound of the rain on the roof would have the same effect. There was no shortage of kids in Morris Cove. Just about everywhere you went you would run into someone you knew. In fact they were so abundant we switched best friends as often as we changed underwear.

One particular spring day, I was with a friend of mine named Twig. He was an interesting character, about 5' tall with a mop of hair on his head weighing approximately 19 ½ lbs. that would put Elvis to shame. Twig saw himself differently than others saw him. When you looked at him you saw a skinny little kid no bigger than an actual twig, but his perception of himself was different. When he looked at himself he saw Hulk Hogan, Arnold Schwarzenegger and Chuck Norris rolled into one. He actually reminded me of a skinny version of that crazy cartoon character the Tasmanian Devil. He was the type of kid that was always looking for some kind of action. With a pack of Viceroy cigarettes rolled up in the sleeve of his t-shirt and his pegged pants clutching his ankles in a death grip, Twig was a perfect poster boy for the juvenile delinquent so in vogue at that time.

On this day, Twig and I were walking

along the seawall not going anywhere in particular. I remember it clearly, it was mid-morning, and suddenly Twig reached down and picked up a matchbook. In those days matchbooks had advertisements on them. This one had an ad designed to convince people to sell shoes in their spare time. Without really thinking about it, I turned to him and said, "You know what would be funny? Why don't we send away for this and have it sent to Mayche's house? Mayche was probably my best friend at the time. He lived on Woodward Avenue which led directly into Fort Hale Park. We were both born in Morris Cove (Twig was a transplant) so I had known Mayche most of my life, and he was the perfect person to play a prank on.

We immediately went to my house and filled out the appropriate information needed to begin Mayche on the road to starting his own shoe business. We mailed it, sat back and waited.

About two weeks later, Twig and I were in Ralph's Park Gate Spa having forgotten all about our little scheme. Twig was playing the pinball machine, I was sitting at the counter nursing a Coke when in walked Mayche. He went directly to the pinball machine and silently watched Twig working the flippers like a pro. He said nothing for several minutes and then as sort of an afterthought he said, "Hey, I got this crazy shoe kit in the mail today. I have no idea what it is or why it was sent to me, I didn't order it, but if

I don't return it in 5 to 7 days I have to pay for it, and its gonna cost me to mail it back." Twig and I were busting a seam trying not to laugh. Just one snicker, one giggle would tip our hand. We waited until we were outside away from Mayche then we let loose doubling over and laughing hysterically. It was then the thought popped into my head, why not keep this thing going?

That very afternoon Twig and I went to work collecting matchbook covers with ads on them. As fast as we found them, we sent them off addressed to Mayche's house. There were all kinds of "get rich quick" schemes. Everything from selling real-estate to learning to fly an airplane. Some of them even involved live animals! Sea monkeys, turtles, even baby alligators. One particular favorite of mine, was a book entitled, "How To Train Horses In Your Spare Time." I think the reason this appealed to me was because for some unknown reason Mayche's father had a picture of a horse painted on the door of his pick up truck. In any case I thought it was funny. All sorts of things started to arrive in the mail at a feverish pace. Of course this was costing Mayche a lot of money in return postage. Every time we saw him he was complaining about some crazy thing he received in the mail. "If I ever get my hands on whoever is sending me this stuff, I'll cripple 'em." Twig and I just remained calm and tried as hard as we could to keep a straight face. In the mean time new "matchbook opportunities" were pouring in. "Become a Notary Public, Learn Taxidermy In Your Spare Time, Sell Greeting Cards, How To Raise Chinchillas For Fun And Profit." The list was endless.

Weeks went by. Mayche's inventory was growing. Almost every day things were arriving at his house. Bob the mailman was getting tired delivering the latest "opportunities" that would send Mayche into a higher tax bracket. With each new delivery, the smoke coming out of Mayche's ears grew more intense. Twig and I were starting to become a little concerned. What if he found out that we were the culprits? True, the chances were slim, but what if by some freak coincidence he did find out it was us? After thinking about it we decided to relax, there was no way he could ever find out unless one of us were to panic and rat the other one out and the chances of that were slim and none. As it turned out our worst fears were realized.

It was a Sunday morning. Church had just let out and the Spa was bustling with customers. Twig was at his usual post at the pinball machine and I was flipping through an Archie comic book when Mayche came in. He seemed uncharacteristically calm. We sensed something was up but tried not to let on. He said nothing, but we knew, he knew. I started to sweat, I felt my face getting flush. It was just a matter of time. Finally he spoke. His words were calm and gentle…"You. And you." he said pointing. Twig and I looked at each other knowing the ax had fallen. Mayche continued, "You two are the ones who have been sending me all of that stuff in the mail. Don't deny it, I know it's you." Somehow, someway he had figured it out. But how? We had left no paper trail, no tell tail clues, no sloppy mistakes. We had covered our tracks, neither of us told anyone else. How did he find out? There was just one thing to do. Fess-up. There was no way out, he knew the truth. It would do us no good to deny it. In fact, it would only make matters worse. "Mayche," I said, "You got us…we confess. But how did you know it was us? How did you figure it out?"

Its funny how sometimes we find ourselves hanging on the very gallows we have built for someone else. What we thought was the perfect crime turned out to be our own undoing. Unbeknownst to us one of the things we sent Mayche was a book entitled, "How To Be A Detective." Chapter one was "Using the process of elimination." Mayche read the book! He applied the methods taught therein, and by the process of elimination he figured out who the culprits were. He painstakingly went through the names of every possible suspect he could think of and one by one eliminated them until Twig and I were the only ones left. There we were, naked, hanging on our own gallows for all the world to see. Once again justice had been served, the right prevailed, the bad guys lost. In the end Mayche had outsmarted us.

Every now and then, in the wee small hours of the morning, I'll hear the sound of distant thunder or the rain on the roof and I am taken back to a happier, simpler time. I think of my days growing up in Morris Cove and I wonder what happened to all of those people I knew so long ago. Ralph Turcio died just recently (he was 92) and Twig passed away many years ago. But there were so many others and so many memories. I think about walking along the seawall or the sound of the stockcars echoing across the harbor and there I am, back in the Cove, back in my home town. And I think to myself, "I wonder what Bob the mailman is bringing Mayche today."

Chapter Two

Tweed

Whenever I look back through the prism of time to my youth and growing up in Morris Cove it seems to me that I always had a dog. I'm sure there were many dogs through the years most of them long forgotten. There is one however that stands out in my mind more than any of the others. His name was Chubby. Identifying the exact breed of Chubby is not easy. He was sort of a combination between a German Sheppard and a Collie with a little bit of wolf thrown in. Back then he was considered a mutt. I don't think that term is used anymore. Political correctness even extends to the animal world. I personally don't have anything against cats, but I recognized from very early on that I was definitely a dog man. It seems to me that boys own dogs, and cats own girls, but no one owns a cat. The difference between them is, a dog appreciates just about anything you do for them. You feed them, you bathe them, you take them for walks, you pet them, and they think you are a god! A cat is different. You feed them, you pet them and they think *they* are a god! Let's face it, it's a cat's world, we just live in it.

Chubby went everywhere I went. He just

tagged along. He would run along beside me as I rode my Schwinn bicycle through the streets of the Cove. He was never on a leash, he just went wherever he wanted to go. I remember looking back over my shoulder as I rode and seeing Chubby running behind me like Roy Roger's wonder dog Bullet. I never worried about what Chubby ate. There was none of this gourmet dog food. Chubby wouldn't have known a porterhouse steak from a piece of flannel. In fact, I don't think they even had gourmet dog food back then, he would eat anything and drink anything. I remember coming home from school one day only to discover Chubby had eaten an entire dessert boot laces and all! Chubby lived under our back porch. He never came inside and he never wanted to. Chubby and I were best friends and he never held a grudge. Sometimes I would become preoccupied with my "kid stuff" and I would ignore him for days at a time. When I did pay attention to him again, he'd jump on me, lick me, and love me just as if nothing happened. For some unknown reason Chubby thought I was the kind of person I wanted myself to be.

Not far from my house on Burr Street, maybe a half a mile away, was Tweed New Haven Airport. A small airport, but it had several major airlines that would arrive and depart on a daily basis. However, by far the majority of airplanes were of the Piper-Cub variety. Many a night I was lulled to sleep listening to the sound of these little planes taking off and landing in the distance. Sometimes on Saturdays some of us kids would kill an entire day just hanging around the airport hanger. Of course security in those days was basically non-existent compared to today. People were allowed to walk right on to the runway to wave goodbye to loved ones.

I remember an incident that happened at Tweed that will forever be stamped in my memory. For several weeks, I had been hanging around with a kid in the neighborhood named Andy DiMatto. It's funny how kids will sort of shift best friends every couple of months. For three months, I would be best friends with Ronnie Powers. We would be inseparable. Then for no apparent reason, I would suddenly switch to Louie Landino or one of the Carlson brothers, while Ronnie Powers became inseparable with Andy DiMatto. It was sort of a "rotation friendship" that kept things fresh. I think many grownups practice this same technique today only we're not as obvious about it. That particular Saturday dawned bright and sunny, I got up, choked down some Post Sugar Pops and headed out the door, Chubby in hot pursuit. I headed for Andy's house since he was in the rotation at that particular time. In those days when you arrived at someone's house, you never rang the doorbell: You literally "called" them. Not on a cell phone or even a regular phone, but you stood outside their house and started calling…"Oh Andyeeeee," or, "Oh Ronieeeee," and waited for them to come out. It was strictly a kid thing. I could never conceive of my parents standing outside my Aunt Theresa's house calling "Oh Theresaaaaa, can you come out?"

Within seconds, Andy appeared and we were off to nowhere in particular. As was so often the case we just sort of wandered around. We had no plans. Whatever happened, happened. We rode our bikes around the Cove, stopping every once in a while and just horsed around like kids do. We stopped at Fort Hale Park, and got a drink of water from the fountain, then we proceeded to Tweed New Haven Airport. Maybe, a Delta plane was coming in or we could just watch the Piper-Cubs land. Across the runway, on the other side of the airport, was East Haven. It was an actual town, with stores, movie theaters, banks, ice cream parlors, and drug stores. I can't remember who made the suggestion but we decided to head over there. Andy said, "Instead of going around the long way why not cut through the airport? It will save time" It seemed like a good idea so off we went. For some reason which remains a mystery to this very day we decided to leave our bikes and walk across the runway. The landing strip was empty, there were no planes coming in or taking off, so the three of us Andy, Chubby, and myself headed out across the field. I'm sure there were people in the tower as well as mechanics and airport personnel all over the place but amazingly, no one tried to stop us.

We got about halfway across the field when suddenly, right above our heads, appeared a Piper-Cub trying to land. We didn't even hear it coming. We just looked up and there it was! We could see the pilot, clear as day, waving his arms, franticly trying to signal us to get out of the way. We were directly in the line of his approach. We didn't know where to go, we just started running around in circles. Chubby thought we were playing some sort of a game and started nipping at our heals, wagging his tail furiously and barking like he was singing along to Who Let The Dogs Out. The Piper-cub kept buzzing us but no matter which direction we ran we seemed to still be in it's way. Finally, frustrated, he gave up and flew away. We watch him climb higher and higher until he was just a tiny yellow dot on the horizon.

Andy and I didn't know if we should continue across the field or turn back. That decision would soon be made for us. In the distance, we saw a golf cart type vehicle heading our way. For a split second we toyed with the idea of running but we realized it would be a fruitless endeavor. We were caught red handed and there was no way out! All three of us were instructed to climb aboard the golf cart and we were escorted back to the main building, where certain death awaited us. We had actually stopped an airplane from landing! The ride back on that golf cart probably took only a few minutes but it seemed like an hour to us. What would become of us? What fate would await us? Would we go to jail? The thought of Andy, Chubby and me languishing in a jail cell wearing stripped suits with nothing to eat but bread and water was not an attractive picture. What would become of us?

When we arrived back at the main terminal we were not taken into the building at all. Instead, we were driven directly to our waiting bicycles. After giving our names to the golf cart driver we were told to "beat it." We were totally shocked! Evidently trying to take down a Piper-Cub was no big deal! They actually let us go! Somebody up there must be absolutely crazy about us. Needless to say we went directly home. Andy's rotation was over. When you are 9 or 10 there is an invisible tight rope that is very difficult to walk. Should I tell my parents about this incident or not? We were definitely off the hook. There was no way our parents could ever find out unless Andy cracked. I certainly wasn't going to say anything. And even at that young age I knew they couldn't get anything out of Chubby. So I decided to remain silent. I was finally feeling better about the whole ordeal, what my parents didn't know wouldn't hurt them, or me. Life was good again, that is, until the next morning.

It was summer and everyone was dressed in their Sunday best. I usually went into the Spa after church for a candy bar or a soda or just to see if any of the guys were there. I walked over to the magazine rack to check out the latest comic books and that's when I saw it. Right smack on the front page of the New Haven Register about half way down was an article. The headline read: "TWO BOYS AND A DOG PREVENT LANDING OF AIRPLANE." The article went on to explain how Andy, Chubby and myself had run amuck on the runway, causing a Piper-Cub to flee in frustration, unable to land. I carefully checked to make sure all the names were spelled correctly, they were. My parents had the New Haven Register delivered to our house! There was no way they wouldn't see this. I knew the golf cart driver took our names but I didn't know he was going to give them to the newspaper!

I only lived about a block from the Spa, but that walk home seemed almost as long as the golf cart ride back to the airport terminal. I knew my parents had seen the article, how could they miss it? My mind was in a whirl trying to think of something rational to say to them. What possible excuse could I give them for disrupting the flight plan of a Piper Cub? I pondered my fate. What punishment would await me? All of those familiar feelings of dread that I felt the day before reappeared as I got closer and closer to my house. The screen door slammed behind me and there I was face to face with my mother, newspaper in hand. My father was in the living room doing the Sunday crossword puzzle, he spoke not a word. It was mom who usually handed out the punishment.

After a lecture now long forgotten I was sent to my room for the remainder of the day. I didn't know what fate awaited Andy, but I knew whatever the punishment was, it was just. My mom may have stood only about 4'10" but if I had to choose between her and being chased around the ring by Mike Tyson, I'd pick Mike hands down. As evening approached, I lay on my bed staring up at the ceiling wondering what my long term punishment would be. Outside I could hear the sounds of kids voices playing in the distance. Chubby was probably under the back porch sleeping, having gotten off scott free. Tweed New Haven Airport was back in business. Just before I dosed off I could hear the faint sound of a Piper-cub making a safe landing on a clear runway.

Chapter Three

Plunk Your Magic Twanger Froggy

Andy Warhol once said, "In the future everyone will be famous for fifteen minutes." I think Andy was a true prophet. When I was a kid growing up in Morris Cove there were basically 4 categories of fame. There were famous movie stars, television stars, music stars, and sports stars. Today everyone is famous. We have celebrity chefs, celebrity judges, celebrity preachers, celebrity psychiatrists, even celebrity celebrities, people famous for being famous. The entertainment industry has changed a lot since I was a kid. Back then movie stars were movie stars. They wouldn't be caught dead in a TV commercial selling the latest feminine hygiene spray or Depends. Today all that has changed. Reality stars are now the latest fad. The general public will more likely know the names of the cast of a reality TV show than the name of the Vice President of the United States.

Our household was one of the first in the neighborhood to get a TV set. It was a Zenith and it had a round screen. There were two frequencies, VHS and UHS. On VHS you could watch the three major networks, ABC, CBS, and

NBC. VHS was fun to watch if you liked snow and test patterns. Today we have hundreds of channels, which is fine, it just takes you longer to find out that there is nothing on. My father and my cousin Tommy climbed onto the roof of our house and put up the TV antenna, I remember Tommy standing in the living room hollering out the window to my father as he turned the antenna to just the right frequency. "Turn it a little to the left, now to the right, hold it right there." Television had become the new religion in America and the TV antennas dotted the landscape like crosses on churches.

Saturday mornings were chock full of westerns. I remember one Christmas Santa brought me a complete cowboy outfit complete with two six guns, a red cowboy hat, spurs and even a pair of chaps! I had an invisible horse named Lightning and after the Saturday morning cowboy shows he and I would ride all over the neighborhood looking for adventure. Lightening was a beautiful Golden Palomino with a flowing white mane. It's a shame no one ever got to see him. One of my favorite cowboys was Roy Rogers. Filmed in glorious black and white, The Roy Rogers Show ran from 1951 to 1957. He was known as "The King of the Cowboys." He rode the range on his trusted steed Trigger, his wife, Dale, also known as, "Queen of the West," Bullet the wonder dog, and their loyal sidekick Pat Brady who drove Nellybelle, the Jeep which was kind of confusing. The show took place in both the old west and in modern times. Roy would ride into town on Trigger and coming in the opposite direction would be a 53 Oldsmobile. They just couldn't make up their minds which century they lived in.

They all lived at the Double R Bar Ranch outside of Mineral City. Each week after subduing the bad guys, Roy, Dale, Bullet, and Pat, would ride off into the sunset singing their theme song, Happy Trails. "Happy trails to you until we meet again." And happy trails they were. In later years there was a rumor going around that Roy had Trigger stuffed and kept him in his living room at the Double R Bar. I suppose someone could sit on him if there was a shortage of chairs. As it turned out the rumors were true.

Another favorite western of mine was The Lone Ranger. The show opened with a field of wheat blowing in the breeze and a familiar voice … "A fiery horse with the speed of light, a cloud of dust and a hearty "Hi-Yo Silver!" The Lone Ranger. With his faithful Indian companion Tonto, the daring and resourceful masked rider of the plains led the fight for law and order in the early west. Return with us now to those thrilling days of yesteryear. The Lone Ranger rides again!" Each episode began with those words and ended with the words, "Who was that masked man?" He was John Reid a Texas

Ranger who was injured in an ambush by the Butch Cavendish Hole in the Wall Gang. He was nursed back to health by Tonto, who had been a childhood friend and would remain the Lone Ranger's constant companion.

The Lone Ranger got his money from a secret silver mine he owned. It was also the source of his trademark, silver bullets. I guess he didn't want to use lead bullets because they could cause blood poisoning. Tonto called The Lone Ranger, "Kemo Sabe," meaning trusted scout. Us kids used to make up all sorts of jokes as to its real meaning none of which were all that flattering. It seemed like Tonto's main job would be to ride into town each week and get the snot beat out of him. Even though this was a recurring theme in most of the episodes Tonto remained true to Kemo Sabe.

Annie Oakley ran from 1952 to 1956. It stared Gail Davis as Annie. Gail was a cute little number who sported pig tails and a buckskin skirt and vest. Jimmy Hawkins played her brother, Tagg. And their was Lofty Craig the Deputy Sheriff. Annie's horse was named Target. Annie was the best shot that ever lived in the entire universe. Each show would begin with her making impossible trick shots one of which involved her actually standing on her saddle while Target ran at full speed. Amazingly she would hit the bulls eye every time. The story took place in the town of Diablo where Oakley was a gun-toting, hard ridin' rancher. And she was a woman! For a female to have a lead in any series, let alone a Western was rare. Annie Oakley was my first official TV crush. I remember having a knock down, dragged out fight with my cousin Paul over who liked Annie more. If I ever saw what the real Annie Oakley looked like I would have gladly let him win the fight. She looked more like Earnest Borgnine then Gail Davis.

Then there was Rin Tin Tin. This show probably caused more kids to pester their folks into getting them a German Shepard dog than any other. Rusty (Rin Tin Tin's owner) was a likeable kid, he and Rinny were the only survivors of an Indian raid on a wagon train. They were adopted by the 101st Cavalry at Fort Apache in Arizona territory. Rusty ran around in a tiny Cavalry uniform. I guess there were no height requirements for the military back then. That little uniform was the envy of every kid who watched the show. I used to pretend that my dog Chubby was Rin Tin Tin. I would ride my invisible horse Lightening over the plains of Morris Cove with Chubby the Wonder Dog following close behind. Much to my disappointment Chubby didn't quite have the intelligence of Rin Tin Tin. While Rinny was saving drowning damsels and capturing bank robbers, Chubby spent much of the day under the back porch chewing my mother's clothes pins.

Sky King was an unusual western, about a former military pilot who used his airplane to patrol the skies of his Flying Crown ranch and neighboring areas. Sky was frequently called upon to rescue someone in distress. All of us kids watched Sky King and we all wanted to be pilots. Penny was Sky King's niece and Clipper was his nephew. Sky flew a Cessna named "Songbird." If a real cowboy riding the plains back in 1890 ever looked up and saw a Cessna over head he would probably have a heart attack.

What made the wild west such an interesting place in TV land back in the 50s was a curious mix of horses, cars, jeeps, and airplanes all trying to catch the bad guys at the same time. Westerns weren't the only kid shows that were on Saturday mornings. There was a show called Andy's Gang. Andy was played by Andy Devine, a gravel throated, former Roy Rogers sidekick. The show began with Andy sitting in a big easy chair reading from a book, "Andy's Stories." There was Midnight the Cat (who played the violin and who's entire vocabulary consisted of "Meow") and Squeeky the Mouse. Then there was Froggy the Gremlin. Each week, Andy would conjure up Froggy with the magic words, "Plunk Your Magic Twanger, Froggy!" (whatever that meant.) and Froggy would appear in a puff of smoke and interrupt the story. I don't remember much about the show, but I do remember Andy's touching closing. "Yes, sir, we're pals and pals stick together. And now gang, don't forget church or Sunday school."

Winky Dink And You was a favorite of kids everywhere. It ran at 10:00 am Saturday mornings on CBS. Jack Barry was the host. It featured the adventures of a star-headed cartoon boy named Winky-Dink and his dog Woofer. The gimmick here was that the boys and girls at home were asked to help Winky-Dink out of a jam by drawing whatever Winky needed at the time. (A rope, a ladder, a bridge, etc.) on the TV screen. This was done with the aid of a Winky-Dink Kit which was sold by mail for fifty cents. You would place the clear piece of plastic that came in the kit over the television screen and connect the dots to create a bridge for Winky-Dink to cross to safety. Then, you would trace letters at the bottom of the screen to read the secret messages broadcast at the end of the show. I suppose that made Winky-Dink the world's first interactive video game. Of course, it goes without saying that scores of kids without the kits drew directly on the television screen itself, many with a permanent marker, destroying many a set. I'm sure the parents of those kids loved Winky-Dink and You.

I myself had to pester my mother for my own Winky-Dink Kit. At first she said, "No way." But I sulked around the house for a few weeks reminding her that Ronnie Powers had one and how much it improved his drawing skills. She finally caved.

Sometimes, I would intentionally draw the wrong thing on my Winky-Dink screen. When Winky needed a ladder to get out of a hole I would draw a cover for the hole. Or when he needed a parachute I would draw a giant boulder to weigh him down. Many a time I tried to kill Winky but to no avail.

Of course, who could forget The Howdy Doody Show. I was a little old for this show but I still remember it. Howdy was on five days a week, it started in 1949 and went all the way to 1960. At first in black and white but eventually color, in fact it was the first regular network series in color. It stared Bob Smith as Buffalo Bob, Bob Keeshan (Captain Kangaroo) as Clarabell the Clown and of course Howdy. The show took place in Doodyville, a circus town which had both puppet and human inhabitants. The audience of kids was called the Peanut Gallery and there was a huge waiting list for tickets to the show. Everybody wanted to sit in the Peanut Gallery. The citizens of Doodyvill were an eclectic group to say the least. I remember such characters as, The Flub-A-Dub (sort of a platypus animal puppet). Phineas T. Bluster, (the grumpy mayor) Dilly Dally, (a carpenter) Princess Summerfall Winterspring, and Chief Thunderthud.

As I embarked on my teenage years, my desire for more sophisticated TV shows began to expand. During my high school years, weekday afternoons were spent with the kids in Philly on American Bandstand. Kids from all over the country followed this show probably more than any other. People knew their names, they knew who was going with who, they knew when couples broke up and they knew all of the dance steps. These kids set the pace for the rest of the country in terms of the latest dances. The Bop, the Hand Jive, the Hully Gully, the Twist, the Locomotion, the Fly, and the Stroll just to name a few. Many an afternoon was spent dancing with a mop or broom just to gain the desired effect. I never did master it. American Bandstand was hosted by Dick Clark a perpetual teenager who went on to become one of the biggest moguls in show business. American Bandstand became such a part of Americana that Dick Clark's podium now resides in the Smithsonian.

But alas, all that is gone. The great wasteland known as television has given way to more sophisticated forms of entertainment like I phones and Xboxes. Of course TV will never go away all together. There will forever be a desire deep in the heart of man for a flickering box that somehow will entertain.

Somewhere in that great TV Land in the sky Ralph Kramden is still sending Alice to the moon, Froggy the Gremlin is Plunking his magic Twanger, Paladin is still leaving his calling card, The Lone Ranger and Tonto are riding off into the sunset and I am riding right along with them. Six guns blazing, chaps flapping in the wind, my invisible horse Lightening with his great white mane flowing as we ride. Off we go to catch another bad guy. The Peanut Gallery is full... Finally there is something to watch.

Chapter Four

The Finnegin Pin And Other Such Lies

Practical jokes have always been a part of a kids life. I was no exception. One of my very first excursions into the world of practical jokes, occurred when I was only about six or seven years old. My Aunt Rose took me and my cousin Paul to Shartenberg's department store in downtown New Haven. Of course, we headed directly to the toy department where they had a section devoted exclusively to novelty items. I was intrigued by the chattering teeth, the fake nose and glasses with the attached moustache, and of course the ever popular whoopee cushion. We were allowed to purchase one joke each. We knew that this would be a very important decision as it would pave the way to days, maybe even weeks of hilarity.

Paul chose a tasteful pair of fake eyeballs that were attached to springs. When worn it gave the impression of ones eyes popping out of their head, stretching down to their waist and bouncing back again. A masterpiece in creative design. I on the other hand, went with something a little more subtle. At first I couldn't decide between an ice cube with a fly embedded in it, or perhaps go with something a little more traditional like fake rubber teeth. Then, out of the corner of my eye, I saw what turned out to be the perfect prank item. It was a soup spoon. But this particular soup spoon was different. It appeared to look plain and ordinary but in reality, the spoon itself was filled with clear plastic. No matter how much you tried to scoop up some soup, you came up empty. The soup would simply run off back into the bowl. I got giddy just thinking about it. Who could I play this fantastic trick on? I know, my father.

The chances of us having soup that night for dinner were slim to none. Everyone in the family liked soup especially the way my mother made it but we didn't have it that often. Should I wait for the roll of the dice or try to force the issue? How would I be able to convince my mother to make soup? I took no interest in the nightly menu and she knew it. Whatever was put in front of me I ate. (A tradition that continues to this day.) There was only one way to insure the inclusion of soup on the menu, I had to let my mother in on my little secret. I lured her into the bedroom just to be absolutely sure we were out of ear shot of my father. I showed her the spoon. She was obviously very impressed, not only at the exquisite craftsmanship of this magnificent item but my ingenuity in picking out such a clever trick. To my utter amazement she agreed to make soup for supper that night.

At the dinner table I could hardly contain my excitement. The soup was the very first thing served. I watched my father intensely, all the while trying not to laugh. My little brother Dennis was in his highchair oblivious to the hilarity that was about to take place. My father scooped up the first spoonful. As expected it just dissipated off the spoon like water off a submarine as it surfaced. Surprisingly he just kept on eating, not realizing he was taking nothing in. Finally, my mother and I couldn't take it any longer, we burst out laughing. I have to say that my father handled it well. He had a good sense of humor and we all had a good laugh over it which only encouraged me to find bigger and better tricks to play on unsuspecting victims. That was a mistake. Having all of this practical joke experience under my belt I decided to broaden my horizons and try my tricks on some of my friends.

The "soup spoon joke" as it came to be known in our household, was not something I could play on my friends for obvious reasons.

I had to come up with some other cleaver trick to spring on my buddies. Unfortunately, it's right at this point that my innocent story turns diabolical.

Hopalong Cassidy was one of my favorite cowboys. He had his own Saturday morning television show where he and his horse Topper would ride the range catching bad guys and maintaining law and order in the early west. I owned an array of diverse Hoppy material including a two gun holster set, Hoppy boots, and a Hoppy 10 gallon hat. On this particular Saturday, my friend Mike and I were playing in the backyard with a Hopalong Cassidy western set which included a plastic Hoppy and Topper, and some plastic bad guys and their horses. Later that afternoon, after Mike had left I realized that Topper was missing. I immediately suspected Mike. He was the only one around that day and I knew that he admired Topper. In fact, his admiration for Topper bordered on obsession. More than once, I caught Mike staring lovingly into Topper's eyes and stroking his golden mane. I confronted Mike but naturally he denied it. I concluded the only course of action opened to me was revenge. I would play a trick on Mike, one that he would never forget.

It was the following Monday while having some milk and cookies that I conceived of a brilliant plan. A plan that would befit a horse thief. I would take the vanilla icing out of the center of some Oreo cookies and replace it with soap! I would also have a secret stash of real Oreo's tucked away for my own consumption, thereby causing Mike to become violently ill and changing his obsession from Topper to the nearest toilet. Immediately I began putting my plan into action. This would not only teach Mike a lesson, it would also enhance my reputation as a first class, big league, practical joker and no one to be trifled with. I already had Oreo's at my disposal and I knew where mom kept the bars of Ivory soap. I loaded 10 or 12 cookies, set them on a plate along with the real ones and called up Mike as if nothing were wrong. He took the bait. That afternoon Mike and I hung around the house, playing cowboys and watching TV. Finally I asked him if he would like some milk and cookies. He said, "No thanks, I'm not hungry." I waited a half hour and asked again, "No thanks." No matter how much I coaxed him he just wasn't interested in Oreo's. This went on for the remainder of the afternoon until I finally gave up. My plan failed, Mike went home and I forgot all about the loaded cookies.

That evening after supper my Aunt Mary and my mother took Dennis and I down to Grannis Corner for some ice cream. I had a pistachio cone, it was the last pistachio cone I would have for a long time. While we were gone my father got hungry and wanted a "tid-bit." Just a little something to satisfy a sweet tooth, he didn't particularly like ice cream. Guess what he found? My father had a pretty good attendance record at work, he practically never missed a day. Now he missed two in a row. This time neither he or my mother thought it was funny. Needless to say, my practical joke days were over, temporally at least. I probably would have been better off buying the ice cube with the fly in it.

This incident didn't entirely cure me from my interest in practical jokes. My brother Anthony came along in 1959 and when he was just a little fellow, maybe five or six ,I couldn't resist playing all sorts of jokes on him. Once, he asked me how he could catch a squirrel? I said, "That's simple, just climb a tree and make a noise like a nut." I will never forget the sincere look on his face as he sat in a tree in our back yard for an entire afternoon making clicking sounds. As the sun became low in the sky and dusk was setting in, he finally quit his useless endeavor. Frustrated and down trodden he went home never realizing he had been duped. All he knew was that the squirrel never showed. To this day, I think Anthony still uses this method to try to catch squirrels.

Then there is the famous story of the Finnegin Pin. Anthony always had a love for Volkswagens. When he was old enough to drive, after saving all of his money for what seemed like an eternity, he finally bought one. It developed some sort of mechanical problem and he came to me for advise. (first mistake.) After consulting the Volkswagen manual I told him the problem was obvious, he needed a Finnegin Pin. Of course there is no such thing. Poor Anthony... he must have gone to every auto parts store in town, but alas no one ever heard of a Finnegin Pin. By the time he caught on it was too late, the word was out, and he would never live it down. One of my more original practical jokes, and one that ended up costing me a lot of money, involved a toy that was popular at the time. It was a plastic rocket ship that came with a pump. The idea was to fill the rocket about half way with water, attach it to the pump by use of a lever that clamped on the base of the rocket. Then, pump it up with as much air as you could, and release it from the pump by pulling back on the lever. The rocket would sore hundreds of feet in the air leaving a water trail behind. Upon blast off you would have to hold the rocket as far away from your body as possible to avoid getting soaking wet. The more air you pumped into the rocket the higher it flew. I remember seeing a TV commercial for this toy that was a masterpiece of advertising propaganda. The second I saw it I immediately wanted one. The ad stressed the point that it was safe and fun for the entire family. Looking back I question how safe it actually was. If you ever shot it at anybody it would probably go right through them.

Somehow, I convinced my parents to get me one. I was in my backyard, behind the garage when Dave came over. He lived a few doors down from me and was immediately intrigued by this ingenious water propelled rocket. We took turns shooting it off and seeing which one of us could get it to go higher in the bright summer sky. Sometimes I am hit with flashes of inspiration that floor even me. For some reason, that alludes me, (it may have been boredom,) I reached into my pocket and pulled out a handful of change. Quarters, nickels, dimes and pennies, whatever I had in my pocket at the time. As Dave was looking up at the rocket, I calculated the general area I thought the rocket would land, and I threw some change on the ground. Dave ran over to the landing sight, picked up the rocket and sure enough spotted a quarter and a dime. At first he thought it was just a lucky strike. Next it was my turn, we filled it with water, attached it to the pump, pumped it up with air and blasted it off into the heavens. Again, as Dave watched it sore higher and higher, I threw some change in the general direction of the splash down. We ran over to retrieve the ship and low and behold, more money! Dave was getting excited. Could this be just a coincidence? There was only one way to find out.

Dave took his turn at the controls. Maybe the higher it went the more money it would find. This time he pumped it up with so much air it almost sprang from the launching pad on its own without pulling back the lever. Once again while Dave watched the rocket almost disappear in the bright sunlight, I emptied my pocket in the direction of the landing. "This thing is attracted to money!" Dave shouted. I acted surprised. By now I was completely broke but it was worth it. I gave Dave some lame excuse so I could go back in my house and get more coins. My parents kept a jar in their bedroom filled with change I suppose for just such an occasion. I filled my pockets and ran back to the launching site.

It was a great trick but while Dave was getting rich, I was quickly joining the ranks of the needy. I was going broke. This went on for quite a while until I was completely tapped out. Finally Dave went home, a little puzzled but happy. I on the other hand began to wonder why I thought this was such a great trick. What had I gained from such a deception? Not only was I flat busted, but when my folks found out that their emergency money pot was empty, guess who they were going to blame? Could it be that my great flashes of inspirations were not that great after all? Had I put one over on Dave, or had he put one over on me?

I saw Dave recently (after almost 40 years) and we reminisced about the good old days. At one point in our conversation he brought up this very incident. "Do you remember that money rocket?" he asked. He still didn't know! After all of these years, he still didn't know! "Yes, I remember," I said. "I guess some things will always remain a mystery." I just didn't have the heart to tell him.

Shartenberg's Department Store may be gone. But the world of the practical joke will live on. There will forever be those diehard fans always searching for the perfect fake puke, or bloody finger. Trying to get people to sit on that empty chair loaded with a whoopee cushion, or to pick up that wallet lying on the sidewalk with a string attached to it. In the meantime, while I'm waiting for the fun to continue, I think I'll have some soup.

Chapter Five

Cove Day

As a kid growing up in Morris Cove I always looked forward to holiday's. Each and every one of them were special to me. As soon as one holiday ended I was ready for the next. Of course Christmas was probably at the top of the totem pole. I would anticipate its arrival months before it came. My brother Dennis and I would start dropping hints to my parents as to what we wanted way back in October right after Halloween. Usually the list would change several times as Christmas day grew closer. One year I received a Lionel Electric Train Set that blew out real smoke! It came with little plastic suppositories that you would load into the smoke stack. The smoke would bellow out and the engine would make a realistic whistle noise as it chugged down the track going through plastic tunnels and little villages with stop signs and an automatic gate that would go up and down. It was great fun for about an hour then Dennis and I became board with watching the train just go round and round in an endless cycle so we started to arrange accidents. We would purposely put a tinker toy on the track directly in the path of the oncoming train then *crash!* The devastation was horrific. Sometimes we would deliberately separate the tracks and get the train going as fast as it could then watch as the entire train derailed sending the engine and all of the cars flying across the living room. That year I also received an entire Hopalong Cassidy cowboy outfit complete with boots and a two gun holster set. The guns were chrome with magnificent pearl (plastic) handles. It had a black scarf with a metal silver bulls head sliding "knot" that could be adjusted for a custom fit.

I remember Dennis being disappointed because he thought I received more "loot" then he did. Upon a close inventory it turned out that was not the case, the Lionel Train Set was for both of us. One gift he did receive was a wind-up toy Ferris Wheel. I never understood what its purpose was. There was a giant key on the side which when wound up would cause the Ferris Wheel to spin around setting off all sorts of bells and whistles. Round and round it went, in an endless cycle until it's spring was completely unwound, finally it pooped out with a gasp. So much like life itself.

Picking out a Christmas tree was always a major event. We always had a real tree, we wouldn't be caught dead with one of those fake jobs. Ronnie Power's tree was not only fake it was white! We usually bought our tree from the Texaco gas station at Grannis Corner or at a temporary lot they had set up down by the Rotary near the Fire House in the heart of the Cove. They always had a good selection and they would tie it on top of our car for free. We would drag the tree through the front door leaving a trail of needles in it's wake. My father would put on the lights then retire to his easy chair and do his usual crossword puzzle leaving the decorations to my mom and us kids. By the way, those lights were not the skimpy, anemic little twinkle lights that we have today. They were as big as light bulbs! They came in all the colors of the rainbow, red, blue, green, yellow, orange even purple. When we plugged them in the house lit up like an amusement park. My father would decorate the outside of the house with colored lights and a smiling plastic Santa Clause head on the front door. Christmas had officially arrived.

About a week before the big day my parents always took us to see Santa Clause at Malley's Department Store in downtown New Haven. Santa Land was located on the second floor, we would ride the escalator up and feel the excitement as we slowly approached the man of the hour. We waited our turn in line until there was no body left in front of us, then before we knew it there we were on his knee, staring into his gigantic red face just inches away. "Have you been a good boy this year?" he asked. (Santa smoked Camels) "Yes I have," I lied. "What do you want for Christmas?" Stage fright set in and I usually forgot what I wanted.

Another holiday that was fun back then was Halloween. There were literally hundreds of kids in Morris Cove, and on Halloween night as soon as it got dark they came out in droves. Paper bags in hand, trick-or-treating on every street, overlooking not a single house. Ghosts and goblins, princesses, and pirates.

Each year I would try to come up with something original for my costume. I would wrack my brain for weeks thinking up all sorts of crazy ideas that would never come to fruition. Finally, inevitably, I would settle on my old standby, the "Hobo." Dressing up as a Hobo (or a "Bum" as I liked to call it) was relatively easy to accomplish. It only required a burnt cork, one of my father's old hats, some baggy pants, and a stick with a cloth bag tied around it's end. The burnt cork would be applied to my face creating an excellent beard. I have to say with all humility, that had my life taken a different turn of events I would have made an excellent Hollywood make-up artist specializing in bums with burnt cork beards.

There were hundreds of houses in Morris Cove, it would be impossible for us kids to go to every single one of them. (every house was "hit" but not by every kid) By the end of the evening I had enough candy to keep me in cavities for years to come. Three Musketeers, Tootsie Rolls, Sky Bars, Chunky's, Wax Lips, Squirrels, and Mary-Janes just to name a few. Inevitably there was an occasional apple or tangerine thrown in along with a few pennies, but for the most part it was a decent haul. Us kids went out as a group so I knew who was who and on those rare occasions when I did find a tangerine, I usually threw it at the back of Ronnie Power's head.

One day that everybody always looked forward to was "Cove Day," It was an entire day set aside to celebrate Morris Cove. A lot of preparation went into it. There were all sorts of events that started early Saturday morning usually in mid-Summer. Cove Day started with a parade. The entire main street, Townsend Avenue leading down to the Sea Wall was closed. Little girls would decorate their baby doll carriages with crepe paper and streamers. The boys would do the same with their bicycles sometimes attaching playing cards to the spokes with cloths pins to make them sound like motorcycles. Moms would pull their children in decorated American Flyer wagons, there would be floats and the Nathan Hale Grammar School Band would march.

After the parade the events would start. There would be swimming races, boat races, and running races. A pie eating contest and a sack race. There were even less skillful races like carrying an egg on a spoon in your mouth. Or the ever popular wheel barrow race, where one person would lift another person by their legs and try to walk across the finish line on their hands. Prizes and trophies were given out throughout the day. People would be jumping off the seawall into the water in between the swimming races. There were hot dogs, cotton candy, ice cream, and soda venders everywhere. Grandmas and Grandpas would be sitting in lawn chairs under shade trees watching the races. This went on throughout the day until dusk.

Buddy Marcetti was the best athlete in the Cove. He won every race, swimming, or running it made no difference. He reminded me of that Road Runner cartoon leaving Wiley Coyote in the dust with just a streak of light. Once I actually challenged him to a running race. I was known as a pretty fast runner and through the encouragement of others I was convinced that I could beat Buddy. Cove day was approaching so I went into training. I challenged all of my friends and I won every time. The fact that most of them were fat and out of shape did not play into my thinking. I was feeling confident that I could beat Buddy. Just to insure victory I came up with a plan. I would wait until right after the 50 yard dash which I knew Buddy would win, then I would make my move.

Cove Day arrived bright and sunny and I couldn't wait for the afternoon races to begin. I could have entered the 50 yard dash and tried for a trophy but I wasn't taking any chances, I wanted to be sure Buddy was sufficiently exhausted thereby insuring my victory. "Oh what a tangled web we weave, when first we practice to deceive." I waited at the finish line and as expected Buddy won the race hands down. He was standing bent over resting his hands on his knees and gasping for breath. I decided this would be a good time to approach him. "Hey Buddy," I yelled. "I'll race you." He looked at me in disbelief, "Are you crazy? I'm *tired*" he replied. His face was red as a beet and sweat was pouring down his face. "I thought you would chicken out." I said. As anyone over the age of 8 knows, that is the one remark that cannot be tolerated by any kid. "OK fast Eddie," Buddy replied, sarcasm dripping from his every word. "Let's go!" We walked back to the starting line. By this time everyone had moved on to the next event so it was just Buddy, myself and Ronnie Powers. We lined up toe to toe as Ronnie counted down, "On your mark…get set…GO!

They say that the blink of an eye takes 300 to 400 milliseconds or 3/10ths to 4/10ths of a second. I blinked once and Buddy was gone. All I saw was a flash of light. In fact, I thought someone had taken a photo using a flashbulb. I stood at the starting line dazed and confused. By the time I realized what had happened, Buddy was somewhere in the south of Spain. I spent the rest of the day watching the rest of the races, just Ronnie, me, and Wiley Coyote.

In the evening, the action would shift to the Rotary down by the Fire House where there would be a block dance. Local bands would be featured while everyone danced under white Christmas lights and Chinese lanterns that were hung under the night sky. I would go home exhausted after a full day of exuberant celebrating.
Cove Day was over, but the memories would remain.

I know its become a cliché' but those really were the good ol' days. A time of innocence and fun. Our world has become a cynical place where much of what is bad has become good and visa-versa. I suppose somewhere in this world there is still a Cove Day or a reasonable facsimile but they are few and far between. Santa still sits on his throne but he is slouching. We have replaced innocence with sophistication and magic and wonder with being "cutting edge." I just recently found out there was no such thing as the Easter Bunny and I'm not sure I am any the wiser for it.

Chapter Six

Fort Hale Park

At the main entrance to Fort Hale Park are two stone pillars. They seemed gigantic when I was a kid, but in reality they're probably only about 6' high. The Saturday morning before Easter, a chain was stretched across the entrance to keep cars from entering. It was time for the annual Easter Egg Hunt. Kids would start lining up well before 7 AM, and by 8 there were probably about 100 of them chomping at the bit to start the mad rush to collect as many chocolate eggs as their shopping bags could hold.
Ralph Turcio, who owned Ralph's Park Gate Spa was one of the organizers and every year without exception it went as smooth as silk. This event was something we looked forward to for weeks. Finally, when the day arrived anticipation was at a fever pitch.

The kids were separated into two groups. The first group were the little guys, in fact they were so young that their parents had to run along with them and in most cases help them pick up the eggs. All of their eggs were hidden at the very beginning of the park and were in plain sight. They were casually tossed on the grass and were wrapped in gleaming tinfoil, gold, silver, blue, green and red as they dotted the landscape like little jewels sparkling in the morning sunlight. I can't remember being part of this group but I'm sure I was. For the older kids the stakes were much higher. We were held back until all of the little guys were safely out of the way. We were then corralled into a tight, shoulder to shoulder mob, between the chain at the stone pillars and two wooden barricades. The plan was for the barricades to be moved out of the way and then wait for a whistle to blow before we took off. Of course, as soon as the barricades were moved, it was a stampede! We never even heard a whistle.

I have never been to Pamplona Spain for the annual Running of the Bulls, but I know what it must be like. The second those barricades came down we were off and running. Sweat pouring from every pore, hearts pumping feverishly, eyes bulging, clutching our shopping bags with a death grip. We ran for our lives fearful that we would be trampled from behind. I ran so fast smoke poured out of the ventilation ports of my Keds. The noise was deafening as the kids screamed and clawed there way to the main area of Fort Hale Park and the mother load of chocolate covered marshmallow eggs. This was not for the faint of heart.

These eggs were harder to find. There were a few spewn on the ground within easy view but most of them were hidden behind rocks, under leaves, behind trees, and high up on branches. Sometimes, Ralph and his crew would get really creative and hide an egg so well that nobody ever did find it. To this day there are probably several dozen chocolate eggs, long disintegrated, that never saw the light of day and are still well hidden in the bowels of Fort Hale Park.

Each year there was one special egg that was always hidden in a cleaver spot. It had a beautiful gold tinfoil wrapping and was clearly marked Grand Prize. I was never fortunate enough to find the grand prize egg. If I had, I would have received a glorious Easter basket complete with a stuffed Easter Bunny and filled with jelly beans and assorted candies. It didn't take long for all of the eggs to be found. In a matter of minutes the park had been stripped clean like a swarm of locust had just come through. Leaving in their wake, trampled grass and empty chocolate egg wrappers. Occasionally, I would go back into the park later that afternoon after the crowds had left and I would come across a stray egg that had somehow been missed but that didn't happen very often.

Each year I gathered enough chocolate eggs to keep me sick for weeks to come. Especially one year when I was following Ronnie Powers. He was ahead of me so naturally he was under the impression that he was going to find more eggs than me. What he didn't know was that his shopping bag had sprung a leak. In the wake of his feverish attempt to beat me to the punch, he had snagged his bag on a tree branch and punctured it. Tearing a gaping hole in the bottom of the bag the eggs just dropped out one at a time. I simply lagged behind for a few feet and picked them up like Hansel and Gretel picking up bread crumbs. Like I said, this was not for the faint of heart.

Another attraction at Fort Hale Park was the Initial Tree. Actually, there were two of them. Both of them were beautiful, one larger than the other. They obviously had been there for many, many years. There were so many initials on them that it was difficult to find a space to carve new ones. Some of them were hard to read having been swollen and distorted as the tree grew over the years. Many of the initials were accompanied by all sorts of creative drawings and carvings, hearts with arrows through them, daggers, and some questionable carvings that didn't leave much to the imagination. Many a young mother, taking a leisurely stroll in the park with their young child, would find themselves shielding their eyes to avoid them seeing something that would be embarrassing to explain.

The higher up on the tree you went the thinner the branches and more sophisticated the carvings. This was due to the fact that the older kids could climb higher. Sometimes, I would just stand there and look at those initials and wonder where all those people were now. If J.M still loved S.P or if "forever" really was forever. Somewhere on that tree my own father had carved his name vowing his unfailing love to my mother. I was never able to find it. All of us kids made feeble attempts to carve our own initials in the tree but they were never deep enough to make any kind of lasting shrine. That is until that fateful day that I decided to climb as high up as I could and proclaim my undying love to Natalie Juliano. Up until this point I had kept my unfailing love a secret known only to me and Doris Day who had a hit record out at the time entitled Secret Love from the movie Calamity Jane. *"Now I shout it from the highest hill, even tell the golden daffodil, at last my life's an open door, and my secret loves no secret anymore."* It was time to proclaim to the world my secret love in the form of a beautiful carving high atop the initial tree.

The next morning armed with my trusty jack knife I went alone to the initial tree and my unfortunate fate which led to my appointment with destiny. I started to climb, confident at first, but the higher I went the less sure footed I became. I plodded on, higher and higher until I finally climbed as high as I could. I was probably only a few feet off the ground but it seemed like I was in the clouds. I settled myself on a sturdy branch, (at least it seemed sturdy) took out my knife and began to carve. I had given a lot of thought to my composition so I knew exactly what I was going to carve. A magnificent heart at least 4" high with ES XXX NJ in the center and a tasteful arrow going through it dripping two drops of blood from its tip. I was only in the tree for about a minute when I heard a crack. I looked down just in time to see the branch I was sitting on give way. My knife fell to the ground bouncing off branches on the way down narrowly missing an unsuspecting sparrow. I desperately tried to grab on to anything I could to stop my inevitable fall but ended up with a handful of leaves. Down I went.

Suddenly, as if an invisible hand reached out and grabbed me I stopped short. Something was holding me by my ankle! But what? Or who? Who was it? God? My Guarding Angel? A squirrel? I looked back and saw that the cuff of my jeans had gotten caught on a branch. I was hanging upside down like a slab of pork on a meat hook. I dared not move for fear of my jeans ripping or the branch breaking sending me to certain disaster. There I hung for the better part of an hour until I heard the sound of girls voices. There, walking below, were the familiar faces of Lucille Castigillo and Mary Jane Vitello. Two younger girls from Nathan Hale Grammar School.   In desperation I called out and they looked up to see me dangling upside down from the initial tree like a Christmas ornament. The girls ran home and within minutes help arrived. Mary Jane had an older brother Jerry, and he and one of his friends came to the rescue. They climbed up the tree, unhooked me, and brought me safely down. Tragedy had been diverted.

Natalie and I never did have our initials engraved in that tree. She never knew how I felt and over time I forgot all about her. I guess it was all for the best. I had intended to tell the world, I guess it would have to remain a secret between me and Doris Day.

Chapter Seven

Doreen Randy And The Gold Platted Cufflinks

Nathan Hale Grammar School was a three story brick building. The lower grades were on the first floor and the higher grades were on the two upper floors. There was a small library located in the basement. The school went up to the eighth grade. There was a large schoolyard enclosed by a page fence that included basketball nets, a swing set, a slide, and other such playground paraphernalia. Today, Nathan Hale School has expanded considerably but back in the 50's it was still quite small.

By the time I entered the 6th grade, I considered myself to be an upper classmen. After all, I only had two years to go until I graduated. However, my height told a different story. I have always been vertically challenged to say the least. In fact, even when I was old enough to drive I had to sit on three or four pillows in order to see out of the front windshield, this led to another problem, I couldn't reach the peddles.

So, back in the 6th grade I had not yet reached the impressive height I am now 5'6 ½.

Luckily, baseball has always been my sport of choice. I would have never made it on a basketball court but as a shortstop I was unbeatable. Being short of stature also gave me an advantage as a runner. Compact and built low to the ground, I was considered to be one of the fastest runners in the Cove, a title which I held for several years. That is, until I challenged Buddy Marcetti to race me in the 50 yard dash one Cove Day. He left me in the dust thus ending my unbroken winning streak. On the other end of the spectrum was Al Bartone. Al was about 7' tall when he was only 12 years old. When we stood together we looked like Mutt and Jeff. Every time I spoke to Al I felt like I was standing in a hole. Al was much taller than all of the students and teachers. In my opinion, he was too tall. Having a choice I would rather be short. After all, there was the possibility that I would grow, Al on the other hand could never shrink. Although I was one of the shorter students in my class, I was by no means the shortest. That honor went to Doreen Randy. Doreen stood about 4' tall, she was truly tiny.

In the lower grades, as the end of the school year approached there was always an open house. It was a time when parents could come into the classroom and see some of their children's scholastic accomplishments. In the 6th grade things changed. Instead of open house, the school put on a dance. This was a gala affair and it was my very first official dance. Parents were invited and emotions ran high. One thing we didn't have to worry about was who we were going to ask to this dance. That decision was made for us. For obvious reasons I was pared with Doreen Randy.

For weeks leading up to the big day I sequestered myself in my room and practiced the basic box step which was demonstrated to me by my mother. Over and over, step forward, step forward, step side, step side, step back, step back. Repeat. Step forward, step forward, step side, step side, step back, step back. Repeat. I practiced so much it was hard for me to walk down the street without box stepping down the sidewalk. It became second nature. Of course, if there was any other kind of dance required, I was doomed. To this day I only know the box step.

Finally the big day arrived. The dance was being held on a Friday night and I started getting dressed right after supper. I wore my new gray Easter suit that I had gotten just weeks before, a pair of black penny loafers, a brand new gleaming white dress shirt with a button down collar, and a clip-on paisley tie given to me by my Aunt Theresa for this exact occasion. Careful attention was given to my hair which was combed in a exquisite pompadour. I was only 11 years old but defiantly ahead of my time.

We were instructed to have a corsage for our

date. Mine was a wrist corsage that my father picked up on his way home from work, a white orchid. I was adorned with a white boutonniere on my lapel. We met at the dance held in the school auditorium which also served at the gym. The auditorium was decorated with Chinese lanterns and paper streamers. There were long tables along the wall at either end with punch bowls and little sandwiches on Lazy Suzan's. The Principle Mr. Maloney served as the DJ.

I was nervous but I tried not to let it show. I mechanically danced the box step staring straight ahead counting and unable to blink all the while stepping on Doreen's feet as I slid across the dance floor. Step forward, step forward, step side, step side, step back, step back, repeat. As the evening wore on I became more comfortable and relaxed. During the fast dances I either faked it or went to get some punch. All in all I was having a pretty good time.

It never ceases to amaze me that there seems to be some sort of unspoken law, some cosmic reality, some rule written in the heavens that says, as soon as you start to feel comfortable and relaxed that's when the boom is about to fall. And fall it did. At least I thought it fell.

From his perch on the stage the voice of Mr. Maloney came over the loudspeaker. "Attention everybody, we are going to have a special dance contest. It's going to be like musical chairs only you will be dancing instead of walking. I will start to play some music and you will all begin to dance. As soon as you hear the music stop, you must immediately stop dancing. The boys are to get down on one knee while the girls sit on their other knee! If you fall over you're out! The last couple remaining will receive these wonderful prizes. The girl will receive a beautiful pair of rhinestone earrings and the boy will receive a handsome pair of gold plated cufflinks. Good luck!"

I immediately started to sweat. First of all, the only dance I knew was the box step. This was going to be a fast dance so I was totally out of my league. My boutonnière began to wilt. Before I knew it the music started playing and we were off and running. We danced around feverishly trying to keep up with the music, I had no idea what I was doing. Nathan Hale gym became a swirling maze of faces, bodies, Chinese Lanterns, and colored toilet paper all trying to keep up with the music. Suddenly the music stopped! Immediately the guys hit the floor on one knee and the girls sat on the other knee. Casualties were heavy. In the very first round 6 or 7 couples were eliminated. They either lost their balance or they just didn't sit on their partner's knee in time. One by one couples fell by the wayside until there were only 4 or 5 couples left. It was then that I noticed something.

For some reason I didn't catch it earlier. The music would play, we would dance, the music would stop, I would get down on one knee, but Doreen would not sit on my other knee! She would just stand in front of me giving the impression that she was sitting on my knee! She was so short she gave the illusion that she was on my knee when in reality she was just standing there! This slight-of-hand maneuver gave us a tremendous edge. Before we knew it there were only two couples standing. (or should I say kneeling.) It was just a matter of time. We could not be beaten. We had a reverse height advantage that no one, not the judges, not our parents, no one but Doreen and I knew about. We were crowned the Grand Prize winners! Unethical yes! Cheating, absolutely! But our parents were proud.

I don't think I ever wore those cufflinks. I didn't wear cufflink worthy dress shirts then or now. They sat in my dresser drawer for years never seeing the light of day. But I knew they were there. A symbol of my victory and a testimony of accomplishment. I could hold my head up with pride...I had won first prize in a dance contest.

I felt 3 feet tall!

Chapter Eight

The Fabian Sweater

It's a little known fact, that in 1956 The Five Satins recorded what is arguably the best Doo Wop song ever made, "In The Still Of The Night." It was recorded in the basement of Saint Bernadette's Church which was located directly across the street from my house. I was only 13 at the time, but if I had known that just several hundred feet away history was being made, I probably would have grabbed my Kodak Brownie Camera and climbed in a window just to witness it.

I have always loved the music of the 50s and 60s. Surprisingly, that kind of music is not easy to find, at least not on the radio. What passes for "oldie stations" today are a joke. They play the same 100 songs over and over on a rotation basis sandwiched between the Wacky Morning Crew's surprise happy birthday phone calls and the traffic report. I wish I had a dime for every time I heard the Beach Boys "California Girls" or Roy Orbison's "Pretty Woman." The kind of oldies I'm talking about are the real oldies. Groups like, the aforementioned Five Satins, The Penguins, The MoonGlows, Frankie Lymon and the Teenagers, The Cadillacs, The Flamingos, The Harptones, with songs like, "Rama Lama Ding Dong," by the Edsels, "Sea Cruise" by Frankie Ford, "Come Go With Me," by The Del Vikings, "Oh What A Night," by The Dells, "Have You Heard," by The Duprees, "Once In A While," by The Chimes, "Tonight (could be the night)" by The Velvets, the list goes on. If someone were to start a radio station that played true oldies, they would probably make a fortune.

Morris Cove even had its own Doo Wop group. "Eddie and the Heartbeats." Actually they weren't half bad. They really did hover together in doorways, public bathrooms, and back rooms, searching for an echo as they tried to harmonize to their own original music. The lead singer, Eddie, reminded me a little of Bowser from the singing group Sha Na Na. He was tall and lanky and snapped his fingers as they belted out one song after another trying to hone their craft. Every Friday night in the summer there was a dance that was held at Rascatti's Boat House down by the water in the heart of the Morris Cove. Kids from New Haven, East Haven, North Haven and Hamden would show up in droves just to hang out and dance to the latest rock and roll music. Mostly it was the girls that were dancing while the guys just loitered around watching them do The Fly, The Mashed Potatoes, The Twist, and The Loco Motion just to name just a few.

Saint Bernadette's also held a CYO dance (Christian Youth Organization) each week. It was held in the basement of the church ironically in the very spot where In The Still Of The Night was recorded. There was a small stage at one end of the room which seemed huge to me at the time but I suspect if I saw it today I would be surprised at how small it actually is. Even though most of our time was spent listening to music and just hanging around at least it was something to do. I feel sorry for kids today, most of them have nothing better to do than to walk around malls. Back then there were no malls, just down town New Haven. On weekends I would ask my father if I could use the family car and I would pick up Mayche and a couple of other guys and we would cruise the town, much like in the film American Graffiti. Our mission was to pick up girls, which never happened. If a girl ever actually agreed to get "picked up" I don't know what we would have done.

Cruising through town on Friday and Saturday nights was not the only thing we did to keep busy. Sometimes we would go to the Summit or the Post Drive-in theater. Drive-in movies are quickly becoming a thing of the past. They had what was called "buck night." On Friday nights an entire car-full could get in for one dollar. We would cram as many kids into the car as possible. It was sort of the 50s version of seeing how many kids you could stuff in a phone booth. There were arms and legs sticking out of every window. On regular nights we would stick kids in the trunk and sneak them in. Most drive-ins had a play yard usually located near the screen toward the front. Little kids would be in their pajamas playing on the swings before the movie started. One of my earliest memories was of my brother Dennis and I, in our pajamas lying on our pillows watching a movie from the backseat of my father's Oldsmobile.

When we got to be teenagers we would take dates to the drive-in, needless to say we didn't see much of the movie. When the picture was nearly over there would be a mad rush to try to get out first and avoid the traffic jam. I can't tell you how many speakers were ripped out of their cords, still attached to the window as cars made a dash to the exits leaving a trail of overpriced popcorn, empty Rasonette boxes, and soda cups in their wake.

It was at a CYO dance on a warm fall evening that one of my more embarrassing moments happened. Doo-Wop groups were not the only popular music around at the time. The entertainment landscape was littered with what became known as "Teen Idols." Guys like Frankie Avalon, Bobby Rydell, Jimmy Clanton, Bobby Darin, Ricky Nelson, and of course Elvis. I have to admit I listened to all of those guys, especially Elvis. Many a night I could be found barricaded up in my room, standing in front of my hi-fi, hairbrush in hand, (my microphone) and singing along to Elvis, picturing myself on the stage in Saint Bernadette's, basement wowing the girls.

One of the teen idols of the day was a handsome kid from south Philly named Fabian. Fabian didn't last very long on the top of the teen idol scene. He himself admitted he was tone deaf and couldn't sing very well. But for a time he was right up there with other south Philadelphia singers like Frankie Avalon and Bobby Rydell. In fact I think they are still touring to this very day. Fabian was good looking. The girls went wild for him. His hair was combed in a great pompadour and his features were perfect, he was almost pretty! I liked Fabian, in fact I even had a couple of his albums, I didn't particularly want to sound like him because I considered that a step down, but I did want to look like him. Since that was impossible I decided to dress like him. He was definitely a fashion trend setter.

His main form of apparel was a sweater. In fact it became known as "The Fabian Sweater" and for about a week to 10 days it was all the rage. Every male kid 13 to 16 wanted one, I was no exception. It was a bulky knit sweater with a thick collar that crisscrossed in the front sort of like a double breasted suit and it weighed about

20 lbs. My reasoning for wanting one ran along these lines, I know I probably will never gain the status of an Elvis Presley or even a Frankie Avalon. If I was really honest with myself, I probably would never get the chance to empress the girls on the stage in Saint Bernadette's basement. But at least I could look the part.

As luck would have it the Fabian sweater was featured dead center in the window of Lowenthall's Men's Store on Chapel Street in downtown New Haven. I immediately went to work scheming ways to raise enough money to purchase it. I needed to hurry because my intention was to wear it to the next CYO dance which was coming up in just a few days. Suddenly out of the blue the idea hit me, "why not sell something?" But what? I had no stocks or bonds, no real estate, no insurance policies to cash in. The only thing I had of value was my record collection. That evening I took a quick inventory. In those days records came in only two sizes, 45 RPM (singles) and 33 1/3 RPM (albums.) I decided to sell my albums. I had a variety of artists, everyone from Johnny Mathis to Little Richard from Doo-wop to Perry Como, an eclectic collection to say the least.

I can't remember exactly how many there were in all, I know it was quite a few. Probably amounting to several hundred dollars. The Fabian sweater coast $12.98. One of my best friends, then and now, is a fellow "Cove-ite" nicknamed "Greek." Greek lived on Townsand Avenue several blocks from me. I knew Greek was a music lover so I decided to give him first shot at purchasing the albums. At first, he thought it was some sort of a joke. Why on earth would I be selling my entire record collection? He knew I was grooming myself to be the next Elvis, it didn't make sense. "How much do you want for them," he asked. "I'll take 13 bucks for the whole lot." I answered. Greek's mouth fell open. "13 dollars! Are you crazy? I'll take em!" I knew they were worth ten times as much, but such was my mania, such was my obsession. I had to have that sweater, I would do anything, even take an incredible loss. What price can be put on fame and the adulation of countless Morris Cove teenage girls? He paid me, and off I went to Lowenthall's. The girls were about to be impressed.

Saturday night arrived. It was dance night at Saint Bernadette's CYO. And it was time for me to get dressed. There, in my room, hanging on a hanger on the doorknob was my golden ticket, the key to my future, my Rosetta Stone that would unlock the mysteries of becoming Morris Cove's first teen idol. The Fabian sweater.
I took a shower, got dressed, and finally, being careful not to mess up my hair, I put on the sweater. It fit perfectly. As I mentioned it

weighed about 20 lbs. But it was worth it. I re-combed my hair, using just the right amount of Vaseline petroleum jelly to insure the proper balance between Elvis and James Dean. A half a bottle of Jade East and I was ready.

I stepped outside and headed across the street to Saint Bernadette's Church basement. It was then that I noticed the temperature. Although it was September, it was downright hot! Indian summer. I immediately started to sweat. My pompadour became limp. When I arrived at the church, it became evident that I was way overdressed! Kids were in their summer clothes, tee shirts and shorts. Nobody, but nobody had on a sweater, especially one weighing ½ of my total body weight, with a three inch collar. All eyes were on me. People started to snicker, some diverted there eyes and wouldn't look at me, afraid that they would start laughing. I felt my ears getting red. My face dripping with perspiration. My glorious pompadour was by now totally flat resembling a piece of shoe-fly pie perched on my head. The Vaseline petroleum jelly melted down my neck, causing a pale yellow stain on the collar of my beautiful sweater. The Jade East cologne, mixed with my sweat and smelled like someone barfed on my shoulder. I was too embarrassed to leave, that would be even more obvious, all I could do was grin and bear it. I found a chair in the corner of the basement and spent the rest of the evening just sitting trying to be as inconspicuous as possible. Fabian's teen idol career didn't last long, and neither did mine.

Finally, after what seemed like an eternity, the music stopped and the kids started to file out. I waited for everyone else to leave then slowly made my way to the exit. I crossed the street and walked home, the Fabian sweater clinging to my damp body like Lloyd Bridges wetsuit. The dance was over in more ways than one. Today if you go to the basement of Saint Bernadette's church you will see a plaque on the wall commemorating that historic event, the recording of The Five Satins, In The Still Of The Night. Right beside it there is room for another plaque commemorating my rise as the next teen idol. But alas it wasn't meant to be.

I saw Greek recently, he told me he still has those records. Its been over 50 years since the great record sale of 1958, as it became known as. The Fabian sweater is long gone. It faded away into the folklore of Morris Cove history. And like all dinosaurs its just a memory. Elvis is dead and Fabian is no longer a teen idol. I take comfort in the fact that Greek still has those albums. I've stashed away 13 dollars just in case he wants to sell them back to me. After all, you never know when you might need a sweater.

Chapter Nine

The Pink Virgin

My father worked at the same factory for 30 years, Connecticut Hard Rubber. It was located on East Street in New Haven. One of the things they manufactured were the floatation collars for the space capsules. This was before the space shuttles. The astronauts would splash down in the ocean upon their return to earth, like in the movie Apollo 13. They also made the water tight rubber seal that went around the hatch. If that didn't hold, water would get into the capsule, so it was an important job. I suppose my dad made a pretty good living although my parents never talked about money around us kids. We had a nice house on the corner of Burr Street and Ira Street in Morris Cove. Small but nice. We always had a decent car, that was kept in good running condition. We were pretty much a Leave It To Beaver kind of family. My mom was a housewife (apron and all) but occasionally she would work, not only to bring in extra money but she liked to get out of the house and keep busy.

In 1955 history was made in our household. It was the decision to buy a new car. Up until this point all of our cars were used, this would be our very first new one. I remember the summer evening when my father drove up to the side of our house with our new car for the very first time. I was totally shocked! My parents were pretty conservative so I never expected to see what I saw. A brand new PINK 1955 Ford Fairlane. Actually, the official color was "Coral Mist" but it looked pink to me. It had a white hardtop. Back in 1955 cars were still pretty subdued. So a two-toned pink and white Ford was a sight to behold. The entire family consisting at that time of my father, my mother, my brother Dennis and myself piled in for our maiden voyage. We headed down Townsand Avenue and when we approached Grannis Corner, also known as Four Corners, we had to stop for a traffic light. Four Corners was sort of a cross roads where several streets converged. One street led to the Cove the other led to East Haven and two to downtown New Haven. At Grannis Corner you could find a gas station, the Fairmont movie theater and a hardware store. Many a Saturday was spent at the Fairmont watching Roy Rogers, Gene Autery, Audie Murphy and Randolph Scott westerns. In those days, for about .25 cents a head you could see two features and about 20 cartoons. It was very possible to spend most of the day at the movies.

As we stopped for the light at Four Corners, there were three or four girls playing hop-scotch in front of their house, we stopped directly in front of them. As soon as they saw us they stopped in mid hop and let out a squeal. This was the very first time they ever saw a pink Ford. My father was proud. I was only 13 at the time so I still had three or four years to go until I was able to drive. It's a good thing because my father would have never relinquished the keys to me while the car was so new, but by the time I received my drivers license the bloom was off the rose so to speak, our beautiful pink Ford was no longer new, and I was ready to take over.

I was able to obtain my drivers license through a driver's education course at Wilbur Cross high school. I counted the days until I would take my rightful place in the adult world of traffic jams and forever leave the pedestrian world behind. Finally the fateful day arrived. Drivers-ed was the last class of the day and it seemed like an eternity waiting for it. I was never one to study. In fact I would do almost anything to avoid it. But in this case, I studied. After months of faithfully attending driving school there was no way I was going to blow the driving test or the road test. As fate would have it, I passed.

That evening, after my father got home, my mother pretended she had to go to "the store," and would I mind driving her there? My father opted to stay at home in his barker lounge, doing the crossword puzzle, to him it was just another day in suburbia.

By this time there was a new addition to our family, my baby brother Anthony. Anthony was only about 7 months old at the time. There were no such things as seat belts or even car seats back then so my mother rode shotgun holding Anthony on her lap, my other brother Dennis was in the back seat beaming with pride, his older brother was now an adult.

I started the car and gave it some gas. We lurched forward, the Ford was more powerful than I imagined. My mother, sitting beside me, yelled out, "Easy." I immediately hit the brakes. What I didn't realize was that these were power brakes, able to stop on a dime, and it did. Centrifugal force took over, my brother, sitting on my mother's lap, shot forward hitting his head on the glove compartment which had a little metal V-8 emblem on it. Horrified, I looked over at my crying little brother, and there, stamped on his forehead in bright red was a perfect V-8. My first thought was, "I hope that isn't permanent! What a horrible way to go through life!" Luckily in time it faded. Dennis thought the whole thing was hilarious.

As time went on, I became more familiar with the Ford. I wasn't allowed to borrow the car every night but usually on the weekends, if my parents had no plans, it would be OK. I would pick up Mayche or Sonny or Greek and we would cruise around the Cove and downtown New

Haven. McDonalds and Burger King were non-existent so on occasion we would head over to East Haven to a greasy McDonalds-like bun and run called Jor-els. The so-called hamburgers were only 15 cents each. Actually they were more like hockey pucks with catsup, but they tasted OK especially for a teenager with a cast iron stomach. Once, Greek actually thought he swallowed a piece of meat! As it turned out it was only a moth. I was able to use the car pretty much any time it was not in use, until that fateful day. The day my mother got a job.

Savin Rock was located in West Haven, right along Long Island Sound, it was basically a huge amusement park that was split up in several sections. It had a "kiddy park" which consisted of non-threatening rides like "The Merry-Go Round," and boats that went around in a circle, little cars on tracks, and games that younger kids could play like fishing for a prize in a little pond. This park was strictly for girls and little brothers. Next was sort of a medium level park, this was for kids that were a little older but not quite old enough for the "big time park." Rides that were more advanced but not lethal. Like the bumping cars. Then of course there was the big park! The one with the adult rides. Rides that you would have to be insane to go on. The Giant Ferris Wheel, The Cyclone Roller Coaster, The Wild Mouse. Remember these were the days before Disney World. All of these suicide rides were made of wood, that were held together by termites holding hands! You would literally be taking your life in your hands for an evening of fun and frolic.

One particularly insane ride, was called The Worm. It consisted of a snake-like tube that ran on a rail, totally enclosed, and spinning at an incredible speed. It was enough to make grown men weep like little girls. Needless to say I never went on The Worm. Another ride I remember with particular horror was called The Old Mill. You started out in total darkness enclosed in a 600 ft. tunnel leading to one of the biggest rollercoaster's I've ever seen, climaxing in a shoot-the-shoot splash down. There were several Fun Houses at Savin Rock. "Laff-In-The-Dark" (a mirrored fun house) featured a giant laughing clown's head which was truly terrifying. All evening all you could hear from almost anywhere in the park was this insane laugh. It was enough to make you want to go off screaming into the night. What on earth could be that funny? What was that sick clown laughing at?   To this very day I hate clowns with perhaps the exception of Ronald McDonald and even he is on the edge.

Then there was Peter Frank's Fun House, that one featured an attacking gorilla among other equally frightening things. It's a wonder any of us kids grew up at all! It's not surprising that the baby boomers have kept psychiatrists in business for so long, thanks to places like Savin Rock. But we thought we were having fun. It became a tradition for our family (and many other families) to spend an entire evening at Savin Rock upon completion of another school year. Each year, if we were promoted our parents would treat us to a night at the Rock. On the last day of the school year, the Rock was teaming with students, parents, and the usual rabble that hung around such places. All of us kids looked forward to eating junk and getting sick to our stomachs on promotion night. The whole summer was ahead of us, life was good.

Jimmies restaurant was one of the highpoints of Savin Rock. It started out as a sea food restaurant, actually it was more of a drive-up counter specializing in hot dogs, clam chowder, and lobster rolls. Over the years, it expanded and became a real sit-down restaurant. People would come from miles around to sample the unique cuisine. It was shortly after I had my drivers license that my mother became employed at Jimmies. She was a waitress. Since we only had the one car this put a serious dent in my allotted driving time. The worse part was she only worked on weekends. Without access to the family car my social life was pretty much over. She would go to work at around 7 pm on Friday and Saturday nights and not get home until well after midnight. This went on for several weeks until I finally came up with a plan.

One afternoon, after my father got home from work I asked if I could borrow the car. I immediately drove down to the Four Corners Hardware Store where I promptly had an extra car key made. That Friday night I put my scheme into action. After my mother left for work I hopped on a bus marked "West Haven, Savin Rock." The car was parked in the employee parking lot behind Jimmies. I simply used my extra key, unlocked the door, started it up and took off. I only had two things to worry about. When I brought the car back I had to be sure I parked in the exact parking space I found the car in. Also, I needed to have the same amount of gas in the car that I started with. If I could accomplish those two things I would be home free. The gas part was no problem, but returning the car to the same parking space could be. Many a night, upon returning to Jimmies after a fun time with the guys, I would have to wait until that spot opened up. She may have not even noticed if the car was in a different location but I couldn't take the chance. Usually the spot was left open since it was a parking lot that was used for employees and not many of them came and went. Once they were there, they usually stayed until their shift was over.

My plan was working perfectly. Every weekend a couple of us guys would take the bus to Savin Rock, swipe the car with my extra key and cruse around for the entire evening. After choking down several lethal "hamburgers" from Jor-els, we would return the car by midnight before it turned back into a pumpkin. That is until that fateful night.

By this time my father's pink Ford was referred to as "The Pink Virgin." The name came from a popular movie that was playing at the time called, "Operation Petticoat," staring Cary Grant and Tony Curtis. One day someone just happened to call the car the pink virgin and it stuck. The night in question started like every other Friday night. My mother left for work at her usual time, I waited at the bus stop with Mayche, the spare key safely tucked away in my pocket. We arrived at Jimmies about half an hour after my mother's shift started, unlocked the car doors, got in and took off taking careful note as to where the car was parked and how much gas was in the tank.

It was an uneventful evening. Nothing out of the ordinary, we drove around listening to the radio, stopping to eat at Jor-els, trying to pick up the ever elusive girls and basically just killing time. At about 11:00 pm it was time to return the car. I stopped at a gas station and put in the exact amount of gas that we used. We arrived at Jimmies parking lot and were relieved to find the parking space empty. Everything was going according to plan. I carefully parked the car exactly the way I found it and shut off the engine. But for some reason the key would not come out of the ignition. I tried as hard as I could but the key wouldn't budge. I shook it, wiggled it and pulled on it but it wouldn't come out. Finally, in desperation I gave one final exasperated tug, it broke off in my hand leaving me holding only the "fat" part of the key. The important part, the part with all of the "teeth" was stuck in the ignition. It had broken off inside the ignition, not even flush, there wasn't even a tiny piece to grab on to. Even if we had a needle nose pliers (which we didn't) there was still nothing to grab a hold of, it was in there, way in there. We frantically tried to come up with some idea to get that key out, Mayche even tried to pry it out with a small knife, but there was no way.

My mother would be leaving work in a matter of minutes. What were we going to do? Mayche and I looked at each other, there was no way we were going to get away with this one. We were caught and we knew it. There was only one thing to do. We did what we are all afraid of doing but few of us will admit it......... we ran. Yes, I'm ashamed to say that we left my mother stranded at Jimmies to fend for herself. Somehow she made it home that night, a fellow worker at Jimmies gave her a ride. The next day a locksmith had to be called to remove the broken key from the ignition.

It took a long time for my parents to get over that one. In the days to come I would be riding the bus more than I ever intended to. I rode the bus to school and back, I rode the bus to the movies, I rode the bus down town, but I never again rode the bus to Savin Rock. If I did I would have to go by that Fun House, and I would have to hear that hideous clown laughing. Now I knew what he was laughing at.

Chapter Ten

Fair Haven Jr. High

Nathan Hale Grammar School only went up to the 8th grade. Upon graduation you would have one year of Junior High, then it was on to 3 years of High School. Nathan Hale was a neighborhood grammar school. Everybody knew everybody, all of the teachers knew all of the students, all of the students knew all of the teachers and all of the students knew all of the students. Probably one of the earliest memories I have is riding a three wheel tricycle down the empty halls of Nathan Hale School. Somehow, I escaped from Mrs. Wright's kindergarten class.
Once a month or so, we would be sitting innocently in class minding our own business, quietly reading or dozing off when suddenly, without warning, this incredibly loud bell would ring. It was way too early for dismissal so it could only mean one thing, a fire drill! I always looked forward to fire drills, it was a nice break in an otherwise boring day and it gave us a chance for some fresh air.

I remember one particular fire drill when I was in the 4th grade. Joseph DeTulio and I literally went over the wall. We were carefully instructed to form an orderly line, and quietly *walk* to the nearest exit, no pushing or shoving, and definitely no talking! Of course, the second we knew it was a fire drill everyone, without exception, pushed, shoved and talked. When we got outside we were corralled into the school yard where we stood in line and waited for the "all clear." Joe and I were at the end of the line, it's then that we noticed we were standing right next to the page fence at the end of the school property. Beyond that fence was a wooded area that led to all sorts of paths, rabbit trails, and secret hideouts. This was during my Robin Hood period. Ronnie Powers, Andy DiMatto, Joseph DeTulio and myself formed a Robin Hood Club. It was my idea so I was Robin and they were my Merry Men.   Right in the middle of these very woods was our fort. Why not go over the wall? We could hop the fence when no one was watching and hang out at our fort for the rest of the afternoon, no one would even know we were gone. We waited until the "all clear" bell rang and then we made our escape. As the line started to move forward, Joe and I lagged behind, then we climbed the fence, five minutes later we were right in the heart of Sherwood Forest and the safety of our fort.

About two seconds after the class was back in their seats everyone knew we were gone. What on earth made us think that no one would notice these two gaping holes right in the middle of the class room? Joe and I sat right next to each other and the two empty seats stood out like two rednecks at a cotillion. Of course, we were oblivious to the whole thing. We were blissfully hold up in our fort, stringing bows and sharpening arrows. Just waiting for the 3 o'clock bell when it would be safe for us to go home, not realizing we had already been caught. By the time I got home, the school had already called my mother. I waltzed into the house, not a care in the world and ten seconds later I was up in my room wondering what happened. Needless to say, neither Robin or his men were merry for some time to come.

The years rolled by and one day I woke up and I found myself in the eighth grade. This would be my last year at Nathan Hale, then I would be off to the "Big Time" and Junior High. Throughout that whole year I kept hearing rumors about what Fair Haven Jr. High was like, and it didn't sound good. I'm sure that Fair Haven Jr. High School is a lot different now than it was back then, in fact I went on-line recently and looked up their website. There were pictures of smiling students and committed teachers proudly proclaiming the virtues of their school and rightly so. This however, was 1956 and Juvenile Delinquency was at its peak.

Fair Haven Jr. High was located in the heart of the "rough" part of town, in Fair Haven Connecticut. Needless to say it was anything but a fair haven. These guys were the real deal. We're not talking about Fonzie. We're talking about tough punks who would sell their mothers for the price of a zip-gun. I heard a rumor about one "student" who hung a math teacher out of the second floor window by his ankles! And lucky me, at the end of the summer I would be joining them. As that summer wore on I began to hear more and more horrific stories about Fair Haven Jr. High. Morris Cove was almost a fairy tale land compared to the rest of the world. On any given day you might be sitting at Fort Hale Park and Ozzie and Harriet would drive by. Switch blades, zip-guns, and black jacks were not in my vocabulary. The only leather jacket I saw was the one Snoopy wore as he battled the Red Barron in the Peanuts comic strip. No way was I prepared for Fair Haven Jr. High. That entire summer I sweated it out. Anticipating that dreadful day when I would board the school bus that would take me to "The Big House." As the fateful day approached, I became more and more anxious. Finally, there was only one week left.

Saturday morning I hopped a bus to downtown New Haven to buy some new clothes. A new pegged pair of Chino's with a belt in the back. A couple of shirts, and a pair of "Snap-Jacks." (shoes with a flap-like lever that would tighten instead of laces.) These particular Snap-Jacks were white bucks. Shoes made popular by singer Pat Boone, and came complete with a little bag of white powder that was used to pat the scuff marks, thus keeping the shoes as white as a virgin snow fall. I also bought a tasteful plastic silver belt. It was as thin as a lamp cord with a gleaming silver buckle which was worn on the side close to the hip. With this added touch my ensemble was complete.

Fair Haven Jr. High actually did resemble a prison. It was a brick monster with huge smokestacks, surrounded by an iron fence, giving it the look of a factory. To complete this picturesque scene, it had two horrific stone gargoyles standing guard at the front entrance. As if that were not enough to discourage you, the school had a peculiar odor that hit you like a punch in the face as soon as you entered the front doors. To this day I can't remember ever smelling anything quite like it. Sort of a mix of sour milk, fresh paint, tapioca pudding and urine. Again, this was a long time ago. I'm sure today the school smells as fresh as a babies powdered bottom. But back then, the smell was unique to say the least. True to form the kids were, for the most part, juvenile delinquents. They not only looked the part, they acted the part. Weapons were as common as ball point pens, the language used in everyday conversation would put a sailor to shame and most of the teachers were just as intimidated by these hoodlums as I was. The girls were, in some ways, even tougher than the guys. From day one I tried to make myself as inconspicuous as possible but being only about 5'1" that was not easy to do. This however turned out to my advantage. At first, I pictured myself being squashed like a bug under the motorcycle boots of some punk. But, as it turned out, I was looked at as some sort of mascot. Instead of being picked on and ridiculed, I became the object of affection. For some unknown reason these rejects from the blackboard jungle wanted to protect me. I was given the nickname "Mouse," and quickly elevated to the lofty position of class pet.

As strange as it sounds life at Fair Haven Jr. High became pretty routine. It's funny what human beings can get used to. The switchblade set actually treated me as an equal. Not that I was included in their convenience store holdups or chicky runs, but at least they didn't kill me. In fact, on several occasions they even spoke to me! During Mr. Hodge's history class I sat next to Chet. (His real name was Chester but he wouldn't be caught dead using that name.) Chet was a teen rebel in every sense of the word, he even looked a little like James Dean. One day Chet handed me a note from across the isle, it read, "Hodge is drunk!" I looked up and sure enough there was Mr. Hodge plastered out of his mind. He had this goofy smile on his face as he stared incoherently at the class. Chet thought the whole thing was hilarious! Suddenly, Mr. Hodge decided to leave the room. Where he was going I had no clue. Come to think of it he probably didn't know either. He tried to make his way to the door but the floor was tilted upward. He would take several steps forward then suddenly quickstep backwards loosing ground each time. Finally, as all classic drunks do, he ended up loosing his balance, knocking over several desks, sending books, papers, and lunches, flying all over the classroom.

As I mentioned Fair Haven Jr. High looked like a factory. It was even built like one. A double set of rectangle windows ran against the outside wall of each classroom. Three rows on top and three rows on the bottom. It was no problem opening the bottom windows by hand, but on hot days the top windows needed to be opened (there was no air-conditioning) This was done by the use of a long pole approximately 6' long. It had a hook on the end which was inserted in a hole on the handle of the latch of the window. The latch was lifted up and the window pushed open.

It took Mr. Hodge several tries but eventually he made it out of the classroom. As soon as he left the place went crazy! Fights broke out, music started playing, card games erupted, half eaten sandwiches were thrown across the room, and kids were making out. Suddenly, without rhyme or reason, Chet picked up the 6' window pole, and with perfect aim, threw it across the room like a javelin directly into the giant clock hanging on the wall. Glass went flying everywhere but no one seemed to notice. The chaos went on as usual as if nothing happened. There it was, this huge clock hanging on the wall with a 6' pole sticking right out of center. Chet nailed it dead center. From that day on that clock would tell the correct time only twice a day. But they weren't finished yet. The class was on a roll. Inspired by the rebellious genius of Chet, others in the room tried to outdo his madness. Back in those days the schools didn't have florescent lights. Each classroom was equipped with 6 hanging lights that ran across the ceiling, two rows of three. They hung on an electrical cord from the ceiling. Attached to the incandescent light bulb was a glass bowl, it wasn't a globe, it was more like a cereal bowl with a light bulb inside.

Someone had the idea of crumbling up pieces of paper and throwing them up at the lights trying to get them to fall into the light fixtures. After the papers sat in the hot light fixtures for several seconds, they would burst into flames! Each time one of the pieces of papers would catch fire hysterical laughter would explode all over the room. This was a fun day at Fair Haven Jr. High. Of course, the local fire department didn't think it was all that much fun. Soon the fire alarm went off and the hook and ladders were sent out. The school was evacuated.

From my past experience I knew exactly what to do. Form an orderly line, quietly *walk* to the nearest exit, no talking, no shoving. Nathan Hale had taught me well. Once I got outside in the schoolyard, I looked back at the giant factory called Fair Haven Jr. High. My mind wandered back to those happy days at Nathan Hale just one year earlier. Oh, how I wish I was back in Sherwood Forest with my merry men.

Chapter Eleven

Ah Beets

When I grew up in Morris Cove it was 99% Italian. I was probably 17 years old before I realized that the whole world wasn't Italian. I thought everyone's last name ended in a vowel. Most of my relatives lived near each other. My grandmother lived across the street from us on Burr Street with my aunt Mary (my mother's sister.) By the way, there are several things that are common to all Italian families. You never eat meat on Christmas Eve or Friday's. By age seven you are as tall as your grandmother, and in every kitchen there are two pictures hanging on the wall, The Pope and Frank Sinatra.

We called my grandmother Nonnie. She spoke broken English and she wore nylons that were rolled down to her ankles and black Minnie Mouse shoes with stubby heals. It seemed like she wore the same black dress every day. Nonnie would make her own tomato sauce in the basement of her house using a metal contraption that resembled a gattleing gun. It had a crank with a wooden handle that would squeeze the tomatoes into liquid. I was surprised to learn that not everyone made their own tomato sauce in their basement. We always treated Nonnie with respect. If we didn't, she would break out the "wooden spoon." This was a tradition that was handed down to my mother much to my disappointment.

My relatives were scattered all over the Cove, as well as East Haven, West Haven, and Hamden. Every Italian family has at least one relative who came over "on the boat." That was my grandfather Tommaso. He passed away before I was born. There was a massive painting of him in my grandmother's bedroom which I would occasionally sneak into when nobody was around. He had a naked part down the center of his head. I never liked going in there because it always felt kind of quiet and spooky. Grandfather Tommaso would be staring down with his dark eyes and handlebar mustache watching everything I was doing.
Every Sunday afternoon without fail, was spent visiting some relative which I looked forward to because whenever an aunt or uncle saw me they would shove money in my pocket. Sunday mornings were a tradition. We were under the impression that Catholic was the only religion in the world so we attended Mass every Sunday. Like most Italian families, we had a crucifix in every single room of the house.

After Mass at Saint Bernadette's, I would head across the street to Ralph's Park Gate Spa and hang out until it was time to go home for dinner. Weekdays we called it lunch but on Sunday's it was dinner. We ate pasta at least three times a week and every Sunday, but we never called it pasta, it was macaroni. There was a popular television commercial around at that time that said, "Wednesday is Prince Spaghetti Day!" We laughed at that one. Mixed right in the giant bowl of macaroni and sauce were meatballs. These meatballs were not like the little ping pong size meatballs you get in Italian restaurants today. These were massive botchy balls weighing approximately two pounds each! Sometimes, in the evening, my father would make himself a "sangwich" on Italian bread from a leftover meatball.

How well I remember lying in bed on a Sunday morning and taking in all of those great smells coming from the kitchen as mom prepared the Sunday meal. I wasn't allowed to have a taste because we couldn't eat before receiving Communion. However, on more than one occasion, I would be overcome by my lust for mom's meatballs and I would sneak one from the giant pot. Dripping with tomato sauce, I quickly smuggled it out of the kitchen to the safety of the back porch where I would devour it before anyone was the wiser. It was so incredibly delicious I knew God would forgive me. Even though He was not originally from the Cove, I knew God must be an Italian. Not everyone who lived in the Cove was an Italian. Approximately one percent or so were "foreigners." Irish, or German decent, they could never figure out why all of our living room furniture was covered in plastic.

Back in the early 50's it was not uncommon to see and hear peddlers coming down the street. There was the Ice Man, the Bread Man, the Fish Man, the Coal Man, the Fruit and Vegetable man, and the Fuller-Brush man. Not to mention our usual milk man and mail man. It was a busy neighborhood to say the least. Many of them we knew by name.

For a true Italian, there are five main food groups:
1. Meats
2. Dairy
3. Carbs
4. Fruits and Vegetables
5. Pizza

When I say pizza, I'm not talking about Domino's or Little Caesar's. I'm talking about the *real* stuff. Real brick oven pizza that would make any true Italian's taste buds explode with desire. Actually, we never called it pizza, it was appizza (pronounced ah-beets.) New Haven was known for having the best pizza restaurants in the United States. Probably at the top of the heap was Pepe's. Founded in 1925 by Frank Pepe an Italian immigrant. As a youngster, Frank worked at a bakery on Wooster Street in New Haven. He began walking through the Wooster Square market selling his "tomato pies." After saving enough money, he was able to buy a wagon. He did so well selling his pizzas that he was eventually able to take over his employer's business and turn it into the first Pepe's Pizzeria. To this day, people come from all over the world to sample Pepe's pizza.

However there was a problem. The piece of land which Pepe's restaurant sat on was owned by the Boccamiello family. They made Frank leave so that they could start their own pizzeria at that same establishment, which they renamed The Spot. Pepe moved his restaurant to its current location right next door to The Spot in 1936. The Pepe family later bought back The Spot from the Boccamiello family in 1981 and now both restaurants serve the same menu.

Another Wooster Street pizza restaurant is Sally's Apizza. Sally's was founded by Pepe's nephew Sal Consiglio in 1938. Sally's and Pepe's have a long friendly rivalry and pizza fans are divided over which serves the better pizza. It is a well known fact that Frank Sinatra was a fan of Sally's, while President Ronald Reagan preferred Pepe's. I personally have to go with Frank on this one, although to be perfectly honest, I think its hard to tell them apart. Robert DeNiro, Henry Winkler, Kelly Clarkson, Bill

Murray, Ernest Borgnine, Kevin James, and Vince Vaughn have all visited Pepe's or Sally's. I remember as a kid standing in line for what seemed like hours with my parents waiting to be seated. That has become as much of a tradition as the pizza itself. There were other lesser known pizza restaurants in the area. Tolli's in East Haven was one of them. I probably frequented Tolli's more than the others just because of its close proximity to my house. As a kid we would take in a Saturday matinee at the Capitol Theater in East Haven, then inhale an entire mozzarella and sausage pizza before going home for supper.

Modern Pizza was located on State Street in New Haven. For some unknown reason I was completely obsessed with Modern pizza's for an entire summer. I couldn't get enough. Every chance I got I would head over to State Street for my "fix." Eventually, my mania wore off and I returned to the more familiar pizzerias like Pepe's and The Spot. On special occasions or just when the mood caught them my parents would take us to Sally's or Pepe's for "ah-beets." Usually on a Friday night. The moment we opened the door we were immersed in the incredibly wonderful aroma of brick oven pizza. We would slide into a corner booth and order a large mozzarella (pronounced moot-sa-dell) with sausage and mushrooms, along with a Foxen Park Birch Beer Soda. We were immediately transported directly to heaven. There is absolutely no comparison with what passes as pizza today and the genuine article. I'll take Papa Pepe over Papa John any day.

So much of my childhood has vanished. I remember when prizes in a box of Cracker Jacks were really prizes. Today they are reduced to paper stop signs or little pieces of plastic that doesn't mean anything. I don't see too many street venders anymore selling fish or fruits and vegetables. The Fuller Brush Man is a thing of the past. Most people never even heard of a coal furnace and why on earth would anyone need an ice man? But thank God some things are constants, they never change. The sun will rise and set each day, lovers still hold hands and gaze at the moon, ocean waves still rush to shore, and those two institutions, Pepe's and Sally's are still making those Italian tomato pies. Like two beacons of light on a dark horizon…Morris Cove will always have Ah-Beets.

Chapter Twelve

The Junior Prom

"**I** think Dean wants to go out." I heard the familiar voice of my wife say as I woke from a dreamless sleep. Dean is our Miniature Schnauzer and it was my turn. I opened my eyes to see Dean's face one inch away from mine staring at me. That was his way of letting me know nature was calling. I fumbled out of bed glancing at the clock as I looked for Dean's leash, it was 3:00 a.m. I stepped outside into the cool night air as Dean saluted every bush in the back yard, by the time he was finished I was wide awake. I knew it would be at least an hour before I was able to go back to sleep so I decided to watch a little TV.

Television at 3:00 in the morning is not exactly prime time. I can see why they call it the boob tube. Of course there were the usual infomercials. The Magic Bullet, Veg-O-Matic, and razor-sharp knives that were guaranteed to slice off an appendage with a mere flick of the wrist. One particular infomercial which completely captivated me was a small oven that looked a lot like a waffle iron. The show was hosted by an over enthusiastic woman who jumped from one oven to another making every imaginable recipe known to modern man. She was followed around by her trusted minion who responded with glee as he tasted each item on her menu. Her kitchen was equipped with 756 of these little ovens so her catalog of exotic cuisine was extensive. She cooked everything from fried chicken to crepes hopping from one oven to another without skipping a beat. I guess she never heard of a microwave.

Ads for lethal drugs were also readily available on TV in the wee small hours of the morning. That is, the ads were readily available... not the drugs. You needed a prescription from your friendly neighborhood doctor to get them. Of course the side effects were much worse than the diseases they claimed to cure. You may get rid of your arthritis pain but the side effects included bleeding from the eyes, ears, nose, rectum and eventually culminating in death. But bless the Lord the pain would be gone.

I continued channel surfing until I finally stumbled across an old movie entitled Destination Moon. It was made in 1950 and I remember seeing it at the Capitol movie theater in East Haven when I was eight. No sooner had I settled down on my overstuffed sofa when I was confronted with yet another commercial. This one was for a men's clothing boutique specializing in tuxedo sales and rentals. As the announcer droned on about how stylish his customers looked, my eyes became heavy. I started to drift off to sleep. In the twilight of my subconscious I remembered a time so very long ago when I was introduced to my very first rented tux.

Let's face it, girls mature much faster than boys. By the age of nine girls are wearing make-up, sporting high heels and planning their weddings while boys are still sitting on mother's knee puking up pabulum. This fact became painfully clear to me in my junior year of high school.

By this time in my teenage career the group of kids I hung around with included girls, but us guys never considered them real girls. They were just female guys. We were all from the Cove and we would take turns hanging out at each others houses after school and on weekends. We would listen to records, play softball, or just goof around. Vinny and his sister Eleanor lived on Townsand Avenue just before the sea wall. It was on a warm spring evening, while a group of us were sitting on their back porch, when Vinny and Eleanor had an unexpected visitor. It's funny how life-changing moments can sneak up on you when you least expect it. That particular evening was just like any other, nothing special or out of the ordinary but soon all that would change. I never would have guessed that in a fleeting millisecond life on planet earth would change dramatically and Morris Cove would become a haven of bliss.

Common to most Italian families, then and now, is the unexpected pop-over visit. Out of the blue relatives would just pop over unannounced. This particular evening, Vinny and Eleanor's Aunt and Uncle stopped by, along with their daughter Noreen who just happened to be one year younger then me. It was love at first sight. True it was only puppy love but it was real to the puppy. Noreen was a real girl. She looked like a girl, she smelled like a girl, she sounded like a girl, and she moved like a girl. Most of the girls I had known up until this point were boys in dresses. Noreen was a completely different animal. I was totally unprepared for this chance meeting with destiny. She joined us on the back porch. I tried not to stare at her but I couldn't help myself, and she would catch me every time. As soon as her eyes met mine I would immediately look away but it was too late. I was hooked, the lamb was being led to the slaughter.

I spent that entire evening just starring at Noreen. Unable to speak, I just gawked at her with this goofy expression on my face as if I had just swallowed a June bug. I am sure she thought that I was a Martian sent to earth to study earth girls. The following days and weeks were consumed with thoughts of Noreen. I couldn't eat or sleep, every waking moment was spent trying to figure out a way to see her again. Every love song I heard on the radio was about Noreen. At night I would lie awake in bed thinking of some heroic gesture that would win her over. I was her knight in shinning armor that would scoop her up on my trusted steed and ride away into the sunset. Little did I know what was up ahead, just around the corner. The only communication I had with Noreen was through her cousin Eleanor. She was my life line, my connection, she was the man. I convinced Eleanor to invite Noreen over on the following weekend, she lived in the city of New Haven which was only a bus ride away.

Saturday morning dawned bright and sunny. I woke up early, excited about seeing Noreen. After carefully selecting my wardrobe and combing my hair, (a major undertaking) I headed over to Vinny's house. Both he and Eleanor knew about my obsession with Noreen and they agreed to help me win her over. At this point in my festering youth I hadn't even spoken to many girls let alone asked one out, in fact the only female that showed any interest in me at all was my mother and even back then I knew she didn't count. At this point in my life, girls were something to be tolerated and nothing more. So I was definitely in un-chartered waters.

The bus stop could be seen from Vinny's house so we spent the morning sitting on his front porch steps watching each bus as it pulled up to deposit or collect passengers. Noreen said she would be arriving by mid-morning, it was already 11:30 and so far she was a no show. My heart sank every time a bus would pull up to the stop and pull away with no one getting off. Finally, she arrived. She looked even better than I remembered. Our eyes met and I immediately looked away. I was terrified of her. I had no idea how to talk to a girl. "How should I stand? What should I do with my hands?"

Every time she got within two feet of me my feet started to tingle. Because of my being intimidated by the prospect of having to actually speak to Noreen, I spent most of the day avoiding her. Periodically glancing in her direction then quickly looking away. Before I knew it, she boarded the bus back to the city and was out of my life for at least another week. There is some unknown force deep within the heart of the female physique that automatically gravitates towards matchmaking. As far as I can tell, it's not a matter of the will but an involuntary mechanism. Sort of like a burp that kicks in whenever a pretty girl is in close proximity to a poor unsuspecting clod. The following Saturday Eleanor invited Noreen back, and the spider began spinning her web.

Having witnessed my utter incompetence in dealing with the situation at hand, Eleanor decided that the only course of action was an intervention. She would have to physically sit me down and instruct me on how to behave in Noreen's presence. The very first step would be to muster up enough courage to look at her without looking away. Once I climbed that mountain I then could move on to phase two, actually speaking to her.

My confidence grew with each passing week. By week three, I was actually able to hold a conversation with her. I had no idea how she felt about me. It's so hard to tell what girls are thinking especially pretty ones. Sometimes she would act interested but mostly she would just ignore me. I countered this by trying to look cute whenever possible. Usually to no avail. Little did I know that Noreen was in the process of constructing an intricate web designed to trap her prey and ultimately devour him.

My big break came at the end of the school year. Noreen and I had been involved in our little spider dance for several months. Although I was infatuated with her, I had no idea if the feeling was mutual. I would constantly drill Eleanor with questions trying to get some information as to Noreen's true feelings but she wouldn't crack. Eleanor was her first Lieutenant in charge of web construction and I was the unsuspecting fly. One day, I would be encouraged by some little off hand remark that

Eleanor would make concerning Noreen's interest and the next day the air would be let out of my balloon. I was on a carefully constructed emotional roller coaster headed for the big free fall with a water splash ending.

It was on a Wednesday afternoon. I had just gotten home from school and I was in the kitchen knocking together a salami sandwich when the phone rang. It was Eleanor. She said she had some good news for me concerning Noreen. I told her I would be right over so I grabbed my half eaten sandwich and headed out the door. Eleanor was sitting on her front porch. Trying not to look too anxious I casually strolled up to her and said, "OK what's the good news?" Eleanor looked up at me and smiled, "Noreen told me she wants you to ask her to the Junior Prom." The Junior Prom? I had no idea what that was. "What's that?" I asked. "Well, it's a dance." Eleanor replied, she looked at me like I had a flower pot on my head. "You never heard of the Junior Prom?" Not only had I never heard of the Junior Prom but I had only been to one dance in my entire life and that was when I was in the 6th grade with Doreen Randy. It didn't matter, this was the chance of a lifetime and I couldn't pass it up. I was finally going to go on an actual date and not with just some girl, but with Noreen. I would be her knight-in-shinning-armor and she would be my damsel in distress. My dreams were about to come true. All I had to do was get through the formality of asking her and I already knew she would say yes.

Vinny had already planned to ask his semi-girlfriend Diane to the prom so we thought it would be a good idea to double date since we all knew each other. The prom was one week away, I made a check list so that I wouldn't forget anything. The first thing was the tuxedo. There was a bridal shop on Crown Street in downtown New Haven that also rented tuxedos. I, of course, had zero income so my parents spotted me the money for the tux and any other expenses I might incur like flowers and getting something to eat after the prom. Saturday morning dawned gloomy and cloudy with a noticeable chill in the air. Vinny and I went down to the bridal shop to rent my very first tuxedo. As we were leaving the shop, I heard the sound of distant thunder. A storm was approaching. It was an omen.

Soon the big day was upon us. Noreen spent the day at the beauty parlor getting her hair piled up on her head with something called a Bee Hive. I made a quick call to Vinny just to make sure everything was all set for that evening. Finally, I called Noreen and informed her that we would be picking her up at 7 p.m. sharp.
From this point on things started to unravel quickly. I suddenly came to the startling realization that neither Vinny or myself had made

any arraignments for transportation. Usually, a group of kids would get together and rent a Limo for the evening. I had completely forgotten to secure a Limo and neither of us had our drivers license. I toyed with the idea of calling a taxi but the thought of showing up at Noreen's house in a rented tux and a Yellow Cab with time on the meter did not have the same appeal as a knight on a gleaming white steed.

There was only one option open to us. I would have to ask my father to drive us to the prom. Noreen was totally oblivious to this. She was obviously expecting a Limo. I watched her face drop as we pulled up in front of her house in our family car, a pink 1955 Ford known as the Pink Virgin with my father behind the wheel. As we drove to the dance Noreen sat stone faced next to me in the back seat saying not a word. Diane sat next to Noreen while Vinny sat in the front seat riding shotgun next to my father. I, thinking all of this was perfectly normal gazed out the window with a silly grin on my face watching the birds. We made arraignments to be picked up after the prom and proceeded inside for a night of fun, romance and dance under the crepe paper decorations in the Wilbur Cross High School gym.

Because of the transportation fiasco we arrived late. Both girls looked very nice. Noreen had on a yellow gown and sported a wrist corsage that I had picked up at the local florist. Her Bee-Hive hair stood towering over my head as I proceeded to attempt to slow dance. My dancing skills have become legendary in the folklore of Morris Cove history. When I slow dance, I look like I am pushing a wheel barrow around the floor. When I fast dance, I'm told I resemble Jerry Lewis on steroids. In any case, we made it through the evening in one piece. By the end of the evening Noreen was beginning to speak to me again. It would be short lived.

The dance was over and everyone filed out of the gym and proceeded to locate their Limo's. Noreen, Vinny, Diane, and myself stood at the front entrance of the school. My father was nowhere in sight. Soon the lights went out and we stood in the dark waiting. A half an hour went by and still no sign of a pink ford. I knew there was a phone booth on the other side of the school so we decided to start walking. As we made our way to the phone booth once again I heard the distant sound of thunder. By the time we got there it was pouring. Not just pouring… it rained so hard the animals were paring up! Noreen's beautiful yellow gown looked like wet toilet paper. Her mascara dripped down her face giving her the appearance of a rabid raccoon, and that glorious Bee Hive hairdo now resembled a deflated Goodyear Blimp. My rented tuxedo weighed 50 lbs. At one point I looked behind me to see if my father was coming and I caught a glimpse of my boutonnière floating downstream in the gutter. My father had fallen asleep in front of the TV set, by the time he woke up it was too late, the damage had been done, the dance was over. But prom night was not over yet.

The four of us tried to huddle into the phone booth to keep dry. Finally, in the distance, I saw the dim headlights of an oncoming car. It was him or so I thought. We piled into the car looking like drowned rats. There sitting behind the wheel was my mother. I was about to be driven home from my Junior Prom by my mother. We made the wise decision to go directly home and skip the traditional after prom snack. It is at this point that my mother made a logistical error. Instead of taking Diane home first which would have been the proper protocol, for some unknown reason she decided to drop off Vinny. This made it extremely difficult for Vinny to walk Diane to her door for the traditional good night kiss. We pulled up to Vinny's house, he mumbled just one word, "Goodnight" and he slithered away disappearing into his house. Diane was next. When we arrived at her house she opened the door, got out and said nothing. Slamming the car door behind her she stormed off down the driveway dripping as she went, leaving a wet trail in her wake…like the track of a snail.

The rain had let up by the time we got to

Noreen's house. Cars were parked bumper to bumper on both sides of the street. We found a space a few doors down from Noreen's house. My mother parked at the curb and I walked Noreen down the driveway. I opened the gate on the white picket fence that led to her back yard and escorted her up to the door. I stood there for a moment not knowing what to expect. Her black mascara had now streamed down both sides of her face creating an interesting formation on the shoulders of her yellow gown, like two Jackson Pollock paintings. Her once magnificent Bee Hive hairdo could only be described as a hideous joke. Would she give me a goodnight kiss? I looked directly into her eyes, she looked away. She spoke only three words, "Thanks a lot" then she spun around on one heel and was gone leaving me standing in my own puddle. I walked back to the car not knowing what happened. I opened the rear door and got in. For some reason my mother just sat there. There was no attempt to start the engine or even to speak to me. Why was she mad at me?" I did nothing to tick her off, come to think of it, I'm the one who should be angry at her and my father. After all, they had forgotten all about us. There was no excuse for leaving us stranded at the dance. I just sat there in the back seat fuming. Finally, I spoke up, "Let's get going" but there was no answer. I waited a beat and repeated, "Common' Mom, let's go!" Still nothing. Suddenly I heard the sound of a horn honking. It was coming from the car parked in front of us. I looked out the front windshield and recognized the pink ford. I had inadvertently gotten into the wrong car. My mother was honking the horn and waving trying to get my attention. I sheepishly walked over to the Pink Virgin and got in. We drove home in silence. I never saw Noreen again.

I heard the muffled sound of a rocket ship blasting off on TV. I slowly opened my eyes and there was Dean one inch away from my face staring at me. He had to go out again. I was back in the real world, my wife was sleeping in the next room, and soon it would be time to get up and get ready for work. I hooked Dean up to his leash, opened the back door and stepped outside. It was going to be a beautiful day. Dean followed his usual routine and saluted every bush in sight... Finally I had found someone who wanted me to take them out.

Chapter Thirteen

Suicide Road

Just about every male kid growing up in the 50s wanted to be James Dean. I remember going to the Fairmont theater at Grannis Corner with my mother and my aunt Mary to see East of Eden. I thought it was a pretty weird movie, kind of moody and depressing but, I was fascinated by Jimmy Dean. The next morning was Sunday and included in the New Haven Register magazine section of the newspaper was a picture of James Dean holding two auto racing trophies. I was stunned to read that he had been killed on September 30th, 1955 just a few months earlier while driving to a race in California.

Although I was only 13 at the time it made a lasting impression on me. He wasn't around long enough for the general public to get to know what he was really like, so there was this kind of mystique about him that still fascinates people even today. For the entire following week every time I passed by the Fairmont theater I stopped and stared at his picture outside the box office.

By the time his last two movies were released, Rebel Without A Cause and Giant, I was a diehard fan. I tried to act like him, moody, sullen, and confused (that part came easy.) I even dressed like him. Jeans, t-shirt, and a red jacket with the collar turned up just like he wore in Rebel. I convinced myself that I looked just like him. The fact that James Dean was blond, blue eyed, and 24 years old and I had black hair, brown eyes, was 13 years old and Italian didn't discourage me at all.

My James Dean phase lasted about a year until Elvis came along. The year was 1956 and I was much older and wiser. Its amazing how much maturity a year can add. I was now a seasoned veteran of teenage mimicry. I turned my collar up on all of my shirts. My thin belts were worn tastefully to the side with the buckle on my hip. My pants were "pegged" tightly around my ankles and my hair was piled on my head like a Carvel ice cream cone. My time had come, I had arrived.

My little brother Dennis, having been born a full four years later was still involved in childish endeavors like playing cowboys and Indians, cops and robbers and marbles. I, on the other hand, had matured into a full blown pop star wannabe. I retreated to my bedroom every afternoon immediately after school to listen to records. I sang along memorizing every lyric and mimicking every gesture in an effort to groom myself into the next Elvis. I have to admit that even though I tried to look the part I never really was a tough guy. Peer pressure had forced me into acting like I was one of the Wild Bunch when in reality I was more like one of the Brady Bunch. That was probably the case with most of us kids back then, trying to look tough and intimidating on the outside but on the inside a marshmallow, sort of like a Mallow Cup. Even today, I will occasionally run into an x-punk trying to bully his way through life. I always think to myself, "I bet he'd rather be home holding his blanket and watching Heckle and Jeckle cartoons."

Occasionally, I did encounter real teenage delinquents. These guys made James Dean and Elvis look like choir boys. One such character was named Whitey. It was from him that I had the great misfortune of purchasing my very first car. Whitey's real name was unknown to me. How he acquired the name Whitey is a mystery, he certainly didn't have white hair, in fact his hair was jet black. It looked even blacker because of the gobs of Vaseline petroleum jelly he massaged onto his scalp in order to hold every hair in place. Come to think of it, nicknames were very common when I was growing up, probably more so than today. In fact when I think back to the kids I hung out with I only remember their nicknames. I probably wouldn't recognize any of them by their real names. They were creative names to say the least, like Junebug, Dirt Road,

Mayche, Twig, Greek, Sonny and Leacher. One was even called Poop. I don't want to know where that one came from.

Whitey grew up in the inner city of New Haven. Morris Cove was sort of secluded and sheltered from the real world. Adorned with white picket fences, manicured lawns, and neat sidewalks, a person could bump into Wally and the Beaver and think nothing of it. But Whitey was a different story. First of all he looked like he was about 35 years old. He was only 17 but he had a tougher beard than my father, he stood about 6'2, and weighed in the neighborhood of 250 lbs. For the most part he was made of meat.

I had no idea who Whitey was until I was 17 years old and in the market for a used car. The year was 1959 and I was working part time in a factory in Branford Connecticut called Echlin Manufacturing Co. My Aunt Mary had been working there for several years and she put in a good word to the powers that be. It paid off and I was put on the sand blasting machine. My sole purpose in life was to earn enough money to buy my very first car.
After several months, I finally had enough saved to actually begin looking for the perfect mode of transportation fit for a "teenage rebel." I searched the classified section of the New Haven Register daily, circling any and every add for a used car that would be even a remote possibility.

One day, I saw it.

The add read: *"For Sale, 1953 Chevy Bel-Air convertible, metallic blue, automatic transmission, raked and lowered, custom tail lights, good running condition. $8oo. Must sell.* The add included a phone number which I immediately called. To my surprise it was an auto repair shop. As it turned out, Whitey was a car mechanic. I made arrangements to meet Whitey the following afternoon. I borrowed my father's car and Mayche and I drove down to the garage. There it was! It was beautiful. Every hoodlum's dream car. The popular color for a car in those days was Candy Apple Red. Everybody wanted one. It made no difference what condition the car was in, or even if it ran, as long as the color was Candy Apple Red. But, this was a metallic blue convertible with a white top. Mayche and I looked at each other overcome with awe. Metallic blue trumped candy apple red. This would definitely put us on the map in terms of coolness and girl magnetism. I made up my mind then and there I had to buy it.

I should take a moment for those who are intellectually challenged in car terminology of the 50s, to explain what the terms "raked and lowered" mean. It means that the car is lower in the front than in the back. In this case the front bumper was only about 2 inches from the ground causing the blood to rush to ones head while driving down the street. The rear end of the car was a full 2 feet in the air. The car had duel chrome exhaust pipes and the lenses on the back tail lights had been replaced with lenses from a brand new 1959 Cadillac. Which, resembled two red cones approximately 6 inches long. This was the epitome of cool.

Whitey explained all these fine points in detail. His emphasis was defiantly on the looks of the car never mentioning one word about the engine. It didn't matter, we were sold, after all he was a mechanic, if there was anything wrong with it he would certainly mention it. Besides, how could anything that looked that cool be a lemon? We started it up and it sounded like a motorcycle. It was equipped with what they called "glass packs," a type of muffler supposedly packed with fiberglass which makes it a lot louder than a traditional one. I paid Whitey the $800 my entire life savings. The next day, I went down to the motor vehicle department and had the car registered and that evening Mayche and I went to Whitey's garage and picked it up.

This was the first time I was ever in a convertible, as soon as we drove around the corner I stopped and put the top down. We drove around town in the cool of the evening. The sun was low in the summer sky, the birds were singing, my right arm casually draped out the driver's side door as I wheeled around the neighborhood hoping someone, anyone, would see us. Life was good. I began to notice something strange about the car. It looked good, it sounded good, but it didn't go good. In fact, top speed was about 30 mph and I had it floored! Mayche never noticed that I had the pedal to the metal, he just slouched lower in the shotgun seat, put on his sunglasses and looked cool. I said nothing, recognizing that the important thing was how we looked and sounded.

Needless to say, everyone at Ralph's Park Gate Spa was impressed. I had the coolest looking car in Morris Cove. This was providing me a measure of fame which I was beginning to enjoy. Everyone wanted to be my best friend. The shotgun position next to me was usually reserved for Mayche but, occasionally if he wasn't around and I was in a benevolent mood I would grant someone else the honor of being my sidekick. Usually it was Leacher. I chose him because according to the majority of females in the Cove he was considered the "cute one." This was a strategic move on my part considering I needed all the help I could get in the opposite sex department. We would drive around for the entire evening without anyone noticing that I was driving as fast as I could. I had to keep my foot to the floor just to keep up with traffic. No one knew my dark secret. My beautiful metallic blue convertible with the white top, chrome exhaust pipes, glass packs, and Cadillac tail lights was a pig! The fact is, everyone thought it was just the opposite. Based on the way it looked everyone assumed I had the fastest car in the Cove and I did nothing to squelch the rumors.

My fame was growing in the neighborhood and surrounding areas. I became known as fast Eddie. This allowed me to drive even *slower.* Having nothing to prove I had no reason to flaunt it. Soon the word was out. "If you're looking for a race, stay away from fast Eddie or you will be embarrassed." I knew how the famous gunslingers in the old west must have felt . There was no reason to draw my gun, until that one punk comes along that wants to make a name for himself. There is always someone out there faster than you, especially when your reputation is built on a pig.

Inevitably that day came. There was a new gun in town by the name of Dominic. Strange as it sounds Dominic was actually a friend of mine, in fact we worked together at Echlin's. He wasn't from Morris Cove, he lived in East Haven just on the other side of Tweed New Haven Airport. Rumor had it that Dominic had just bought a 1954 Ford that was once owned by a State cop! It had a souped-up V-8 engine in it that was unbeatable. In fact, it was rapidly spreading through the teenage grapevine that the car was so fast it was actually illegal to drive on public streets. Someone even said it had been secretly equipped with a jet engine! And to make matters worse, Dominic was gunning for me.

One summer afternoon, at about 4:00, a group of us guys were hanging around the entrance to Fort Hale Park when up drove a green 1954 Ford Victoria. It was Dominic and he was looking for action. He had one of his toadies with him a kid by the name of Artie. Dominic came right to the point. "Everyone says you have a fast car there, let's find out." I remained calm, trying to look cool and unconcerned but deep inside I knew that if I ever raced this guy my reputation would be shot. I would be exposed for the fraud that I was. I knew Dominic wasn't bluffing, he had to have something hot under that hood or he never would have challenged me, he was well aware of my reputation. I, on the other hand, held no cards whatsoever. I was all bluff! If a little old lady in a motorized wheelchair challenged me to a race, she would win hands down.

The race was set for that coming Saturday at a place we called "Suicide Road" a straightaway that ran behind Tweed Airport. I was forced to except his challenge even though I knew the outcome and the humiliation it would bring. It was Thursday, I had two days to sweat it out. Word spread quickly throughout the Cove, it was the talk of the town. Moral support was no problem, the entire neighborhood was behind me. There was a natural rivalry between East Haven and the Cove that had been around for years. This just added fuel to the fire.

I toyed with the idea of claiming there was something wrong with my car and the race would have to be postponed. But scheduling it for another time was not the answer. Sooner or later, I would have to face the music.There was one concern that was on everyone's mind. If Magraff found out about the race we were all doomed. Magraff was the local cop that was assigned to Morris Cove. Throughout the years, teenagers seemed to be the big thorn in his side. Magraff played the part of the local sheriff in our western motif. When the gunslingers came to town Magraff was there to escort them out and that's exactly what he did. He would routinely stick two or three "trouble makers" in the backseat of his squad car and literally drive them out of the Cove. Once safely across the border at Grannis Corner, he would let them out forcing them to walk several miles back home. I suppose it was equivalent of ordering the gunslinger to "be on the next stagecoach out of town" except Magraff's police car was the stagecoach and he was the stagecoach driver.

The day of the race finally arrived. As far as we could tell we had succeeded in keeping it from Magraff, in fact no one had seen him for the past week. Kids started to arrive at the race sight a full hour before the 10 AM start time. Suicide Road was always completely deserted. It was an abandoned road that was once used as an airstrip for Tweed New Haven Airport, lined with cattails and tall weeds, no one ever went there except us kids for just such an occasion.

By the time I arrived there were about 25 or 30 kids gathered at the starting line. My supporters outnumbered Dominic's two to one. Dominic showed a few minutes later and we assumed our racing positions with Dominic on my right. It looked like a scene right out of Rebel Without A Cause. In keeping with that tradition we picked Mary-Lou, one of the local Cove girls, to stand between the cars and drop a handkerchief signaling the start of the race. As I waited, a feeling of dread came over me. In just a few minutes it would be all over and I would be exposed for the fraud I was. I was no James Dean.

As I surveyed the smiling faces of the kids lined up on either side of Suicide Road I knew that their cheers would soon turn to jeers. I had no choice, I was at the point of no return. Soon the moment was upon me. Mary-Lou dropped the handkerchief and I floored it. To my utter amazement I got the jump on Dominic. I could see him in my rear view mirror, I was actually in the lead! For a split second I thought I actually had a chance. Then literally two seconds later Dominic passed me like I was backing up. In a flash he was so far ahead of me I almost lost sight of him, my car still rocking in the wake of his exhaust. I was going so slow that at one point I looked out the window at the ground and I actually saw gum! I knew it was over, there was no way I was ever going to catch him.

Many years before my teenage rebel stage I sat in Sister Mary Grace's catechism class at Saint Bernadette's Church learning the fine points of Catholic theology. One particular lesson stuck out in my mind. She assured us that everyone has been given a Guardian Angle, an angel that would look after us in times of trouble. Mine showed up unexpectedly that day at Suicide Road. Weather or not it was my Guardian Angle or some other force in the cosmos, it was definitely Divine Intervention.

As Dominic disappeared into the horizon leaving me in the dust, suddenly out of the corner of my eye I saw something in my rear view mirror. It was a light…a red light…a flashing red light. It was Magraff! For a split second I thought of slowing down but I couldn't go much slower than I already was. For the second time in a matter of minutes someone passed me like I was standing still. I kept cruising along at the breakneck speed of about 35 mph until I eventually came across Magraff's police car pulled over to the side of the road right behind Dominic, it was before the finish line. With lights still flashing, Magraff was writing him a ticket for speeding. I smiled as I drove by, not because of my impending victory, but because even at top speed, with the pedal to the metal, I was still under the limit. I won the race and never even broke the speed limit.

I returned to Ralph's Park Gate Spa a conquering hero. Everyone thought I was using brilliant strategy in my victory over Dominic. I humbly accepted the credit. Sadly my beautiful 1953 metallic blue Chevy Bel-Air convertible with the custom tail lights didn't last much longer. It became the unfortunate casualty of a fire caused by the careless flick of a Marlboro cigarette out the driver's window directly into the back seat. It smoldered all night and by morning there was nothing left but a metallic blue carcass. The two magnificent red 1959 Cadillac taillights drooped like a couple of melted candles. However, the legend lives on in the folklore of Morris Cove annals. Whenever ex-rebels get together and reminisce of days gone by, inevitably they remember the great race at Suicide Road. With fast Eddie at the wheel and Teen Angel riding shotgun.

Chapter Fourteen

The Day I Caught My Limit

I graduated from Wilbur Cross High School in 1960. By that time the styles had changed. No longer did I dress like a teenage hood. I had morphed into a clean cut, Ivy League, button down collar, preppie. Instead of a turned up collar and motorcycle boots I now wore penny loafers and tennis shoes. Madras shirts were all the rage. They were usually multicolored plaids that "bled" when washed. My hair was now combed with a part. Gone was the Vaseline rubbed pompadour and ducktail. Although rock and roll was still my choice of music, it was slowly giving way to folk music. Bob Dylan, Peter Paul and Mary, and The Kingston Trio now toped the charts. Coffee houses were springing up all over the place like mushrooms. Yale University is located right smack in the middle of New Haven so the college influence was everywhere.

I always had an interest in art and drawing so I thought of becoming a commercial artist. Upon completion of High School, I enrolled in art school. As a result of my broader horizons I spent less and less time in Morris Cove. I acquired a part time job and my own car and I didn't see my old buddies as much as I used to. Things were changing at a rapid pace, in short, slowly but surely, I was growing up. I dated a variety of girls during this period, nothing serious just the usual drive-in movies and hanging out with friends. Until that fateful day when I caught my limit.

As I began to develop other interests, Ralph's Park Gate Spa gave way to Bochio's. Bochio's was located in the town of East Haven which was adjacent to the Cove. It was a soda fountain, malt shop type of establishment like the ones seen in American Graffiti or Happy Days. I would frequently stop in after classes at art school and just hang around and talk to Sonny, a friend of mine from the Cove who worked there part time. Bochio's differed from the Spa in that it not only had a counter and stools but actual booths.

The girls from East Haven were different from the girls in Morris Cove. I can't exactly put my finger on it, but somehow they were different. Not better. Just different. I knew the Cove girls, they were mostly Italian, dark hair, brown eyes, earthy and built low to the ground. East Haven girls were lighter, more blue eyes, somehow they seemed taller and in Technicolor. I would never in a million years talk to one let alone ask one out. Somehow they seemed to be above it all, aloof, unattainable. Since Bochio's was located right in the middle of East Haven it was not uncommon to see a group of them sitting in the booths on any given day. I would quickly walk by them, head down, never making eye contact lest one of them would smile at me. They would usually talk low and giggle when I walked by… which made the pennies in my loafers pop out and roll across the floor.

One of my techniques in attracting girls was to hang around with guys that were not as physically attractive as myself thereby giving me an edge. I made an exception to this rule when Sonny became my best friend. He was tall, good looking, and had a confidence about him that I envied. I, on the other hand, was vertically challenged and unsure of myself. We made a perfect team, sort of a poor man's version of Martin and Lewis. One afternoon after class I strolled into Bachio's. It was a typical day nothing out of the ordinary. Sonny was alone behind the counter, other than that the place was empty. I was sitting on a stool talking with him when suddenly we heard the bell on the front door jingle. We looked up and saw two East Haven girls walk in, one blond and one brunette, both of them were unbelievably gorgeous. Sonny remained cool casually leaning on the counter and acting as if this was an ordinary day and not the end of the natural order as we know it. There was obviously a tear in the space-time continuum. I stared straight ahead secretly watching them in the mirror behind the counter as they slid into a booth at the other end of the malt shop. They both had great legs that were so long they reached all the way to the floor.

Sonny strolled over to take their order. What happened next is just a blur. It happened so fast, that to this day I'm not sure exactly how it went down. As they were ordering, Sonny actually began to have a conversation with them. I sat frozen, unable to look at what was happening even through the mirror. Sonny returned and informed me that the blond was Barbara and the brunette was Donna. "Come over and meet them," he said. Immediately my ears got red and my madras shirt started to bleed. Deep inside I knew that this was my one big chance to actually talk to East Haven girls. A moment like this comes once in a lifetime. With knees knocking, I followed Sonny over to the booth and my appointment with destiny. I have no idea what we talked about but after a few minutes the conversation fizzled and awkwardness set in. It was time to make as graceful an exit as possible.

After the girls left, Sonny and I felt exhilarated. A sense of accomplishment came over us as if we had just conquered Mount Everest. We not only met two gorgeous East Haven girls we had actually talked to them! It was then that Sonny said something that would change the course of our entire lives from that day forward. "If you ask Barbara out, I'll ask Donna out." I swallowed my gum. There are some things that happen in this universe that remain   unexplained   mysteries.   Why   the swallows return to Capistrano every year without missing a beat, or how against all odds the salmon swim upstream to find that one particular mate, or why the Mona Lisa was painted with no eyebrows. Some things are forever locked up in the mind of a benevolent creator. But without a doubt the greatest mystery of all time and one that I will never understand is, what ever possessed Barbara to say yes!

I will never forget our very first date. I took her to the Summit Drive In. The picture was The Ghost And Mr. Chicken. I have always felt that one of the reasons Barbara was willing to make a life long commitment to me was because of my exquisite taste in motion picture cuisine. To this day it remains "Our movie." It was an ideal situation, Barbara and Donna were best friends and Sonny and I were best friends. We double dated often and eventually we were in each other's weddings. My brother Dennis was my best man, Sonny was one of the ushers and Donna one of the bridesmaids.

I never formally proposed to Barbara, somehow we just knew it was meant to be, we simply set the date. The date was May 20th and it was approaching quickly, before we knew it the wedding was only weeks away. Everyone was busy making all of the arrangements when out of the blue we hit a speed bump. This particular speed bump came in the form of a letter addressed to me. It looked innocent enough, just an ordinary letter, but when I opened it these words hit me right between the eyes. *"Greetings from the President of the United States Of America."* Although I was honored that the President of the United States would actually take the time to write me a letter it soon dawned on me that he was not writing to congratulate me for my upcoming wedding. I was instructed to report to Fort Dix within two weeks to begin basic training for induction into the army. This of course, put a major crimp in our wedding plans. By this time it was too close to the date to postpone or cancel. The invitations had been sent out, the band was hired, the hall was rented, gowns, cakes, and tuxedoes were ready to go. To use a favorite expression of the caterer, I was dead meat.

Because of my art school background I was able to land a job working for a billboard company. Back then many billboards were actually painted directly on the sign. It was the day after I received my love letter from the President, I was painting a billboard in West Haven and was explaining my dilemma to my co-worker, a man 10 years my senior. It's funny how one conversation can change the course of human events. He told me he had a friend, Sergeant Major Persenperry, who was an army recruiter at the New Haven Armory. He assured me, if I paid him a visit he would get me into the Army Reserves. This was at the height of the Viet Nam War, I knew it was almost impossible to get into the Reserves, in fact the waiting list was up to one year.

Hoping against all hope, I showed up at the New Haven Armory that evening. It was a single floor brick building with a tank sitting on the front lawn and a huge flagpole next to it. The American flag waving proudly in the cool night air. The place seemed empty except for a single light coming from one of the offices. I walked over and saw the sign on the door, Sergeant Major Persenperry.
He was sitting behind his desk looking over some papers when I walked in. "Have a seat" he said. I couldn't help noticing that he looked almost exactly like Phil Silvers who played Sergeant Bilko on TV. "Raise your right hand and repeat after me" he said. The next thing I knew I was government property.

Even though I was in the Army Reserves I still had to report for basic training at Fort Dix New Jersey. We were able to keep the original wedding date, however one of the very first things they do to an in-coming solder upon arrival at boot camp is to shave their hair off. In some of our wedding photos, where I'm standing next to Sonny, we really do look like Martin and Lewis. Myself, playing Jerry sporting my brand new buzz cut and Sonny looking like he's going to break out singing That's Amore.

Life was moving fast, soon I would be leaving Morris Cove behind. I would loose touch with my old friends and move on to new ones. The former teenage rebel turned preppie would soon be a father with slippered feet. One of my favorite poems is entitled The Road Less Traveled, it seems to sum it all up.

"Two roads diverged in a yellow wood,
And sorry I could not travel both
And be one traveler, long I stood
And looked down one as far as I could
To where it bent in the undergrowth;

Then took the other, as just as fair,
And having perhaps the better claim,
Because it was grassy and wanted wear;
Though as for that the passing there
Had worn them really about the same,

And both that morning equally lay
In leaves no step had trodden black.
Oh, I kept the first for another day!
Yet knowing how way leads on to way,

I doubted if I should ever come back.

I shall be telling this with a sigh
Somewhere ages and ages hence:
Two roads diverged in a wood, and I...
I took the one less traveled by,
And that has made all the difference."

Robert Frost

Knowing how way leads on to way I doubted if I should ever come back. Home is just a distant memory, but a memory it is. Those friends that I left behind are still friends and they always will be. Yes, its true, way leads on to way, but someday that way may lead me home again. Home to a place called Morris Cove.

Epilogue

Thomas Wolfe wrote a novel entitled "You Can't Go Home Again." I know what he meant, and I know what that means to me. It means that things are not the same as when you were a kid living at home. It means you see things differently, through different eyes. It means that any attempt to relive childhood memories ultimately fail. The truth is you can never recapture all of the feelings you had back "home."

I went back home once, and to quote another book, "It was the best of times it was the worst of times." It was the best of times because I got to see my old neighborhood. I revisited all of those places that held so many memories for me. Fort Hale Park with the initial tree, the water fountain, the pavilions, and the rocky beach. I went by Ronnie Power's house on Concord Street lined with Oak trees, Ronnie had long since moved away but the house looked the same. I strolled by the Sea Wall and Nathan Hale School, now more than twice its original size. Then I went by my old house on 33 Burr Street, it looked so much smaller than I remembered. Immediately I wanted to go inside. I wanted to see my old room that my brother Dennis and I shared as kids. I pictured my mom in the kitchen and I wondered what she was making for supper. I remembered the day when the sidewalk in front of the house was repaired with a new patch of cement and how I scratched my name in it with a stick. The patch was still there and the name "Eddie" was still visible.

It was October and the air was cool and crisp. Fall was in full bloom. The leaves on the trees were bursting with color, red, green, yellow, and brown. Indian corn hung on the front doors of houses and stone walls were everywhere. Typical of the New England landscape. This was my favorite time of year in Connecticut. Being there brought back memories that I hadn't thought of for half a century. It truly was the best of times.

But it was also the worst of times. The reason for my return was to see my brother Dennis who now lay dying in a Hospice Hospital. Soon I would see him for the last time, although he was now in his 50's I still thought of him as my baby brother. He died on Columbus Day.

With all due respect to Thomas Wolfe I think I disagree. You *can* go home again. Not necessarily to a specific location but to a place that lies dormant in your heart. A place filled with memories that are only precious to you and no one else, and every person has them.

John Edward Pearce said,

>*"Home is a place you grow up wanting to leave…and grow old wanting to get back to."*

In everybody's memory there is a place called Morris Cove.

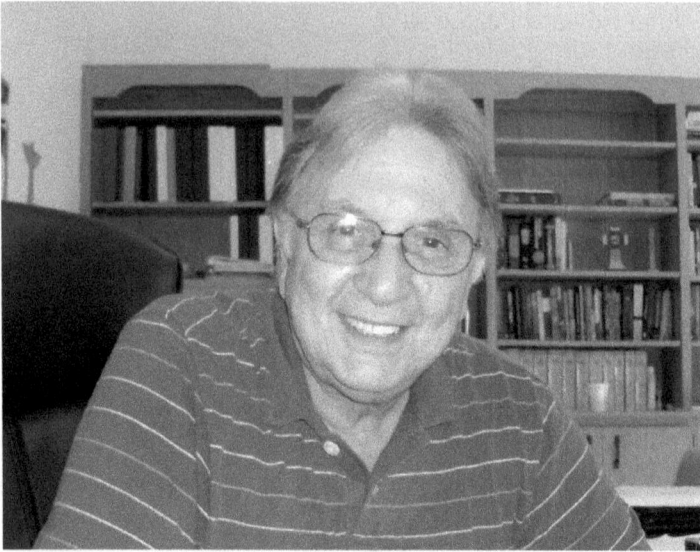

Ed Sabatino grew up in Morris Cove, a suburb of New Haven Connecticut. He now resides in Sarasota Florida with his wife Barbara where he pastors a church. Ed and Barbara have been married 43 years and have three grown children, Jason, Eric, and Lauren. Ed's email address is edjsab@aol.com